PERSONALISM

AND THE

PROBLEMS OF PHILOSOPHY

AN APPRECIATION OF THE WORK OF

BORDEN PARKER BOWNE

BY
RALPH TYLER FLEWELLING

INTRODUCTORY CHAPTER
BY RUDOLF EUCKEN

THE METHODIST BOOK CONCERN
NEW YORK   CINCINNATI

TO B. P. B.

WHOSE WORDS OF TRUTH WERE
A BEACON LIGHT TO MANY SOULS,

AND

TO HIS PUPILS

WHOSE LOVE ABIDES THROUGH
TIME AND CHANGE

CONTENTS

7

CONTENTS

8

CONTENTS

SECTION III

PRAGMATISM

CHAPTER VIII

The pragmatic element in the history of
philosophy—Can the pragmatic test of
truth be maintained?—Are space and
time the abiding realities?—Pluralism a
confession of failure to unite subject and
object—Can pragmatic pluralism reach
freedom or solve the problem of evil?

CHAPTER IX

A pragmatic definition of Being—The escape
from pluralism and absolutism to world-
unity—The ideal nature of time and space
—The pragmatic test for religious values.

SECTION IV

BOWNE AND SOME PRESENT-DAY THINKERS

CHAPTER X

Can knowledge and life be brought together
on the empirical basis?—Time as duration

CONTENTS

FOREWORD

THE essential problems of philosophy are
few. Out of three or four fundamental
presuppositions flow whole systems of
thought. Unless the fountain itself is clear
the outflowing streams cannot be kept so.
The nature of reality, or being, is the fundamental principle by which all systems are to
be judged. Given the basic attitude toward
this problem, it is easy to see what the
logical goal will be. Next to the question
of reality are those of space and time, and
the relation of life to knowledge. These are
the main questions about which all others
hinge. For this reason these terms will
appear frequently in the following pages, as
we attempt to trace the leading philosophical ideas down to modern times, and
to discover their relation to the thought of
Bowne.

He would have been the last to claim

11

finality for his system. He assumed only to clear away a foundation for accurate thinking, to expose the common sophistries of thought, and to give a basis on which to build. In these positions he felt fundamentally secure, being not satisfied to speak "after the manner of the scribes." We believe the future will amply justify his confidence.

This work was undertaken reluctantly in the sense that the writer knew there were many others who might have performed the task more worthily; with alacrity, in the consciousness that there was need to point out the place which Bowne's system occupies in the history of philosophy, and that more than five years have passed without this being done. This feeling was intensified by the expressed desire of Professor Eucken that such a work be undertaken.

The author does not aim at an exhaustive discussion, but, rather, at a brief and suggestive treatment that shall define for the popular mind the relation of Bowne's thought to other philosophical endeavors. To forestall disappointment it should be said there is need for a more detailed and technical work than is possible within the limits of so small a volume. To make a book that shall be brief and yet clear to the nonprofessional mind, that shall drop technical terms whenever possible and yet satisfy the exacting student, is exceedingly difficult. The writer makes no pretense of being sufficient for so great a task. If, however, this effort shall succeed in expressing the deep love and respect felt by one whose intellectual horizons were enlarged by the touch of a master in the realm of thought, and shall lead to a renewed study of that master's work, its purpose will have been achieved.

Acknowledgments are due to Zion's Herald for the use of materials first printed therein; to Dr. Marshall Livingstone Perrin, who transcribed and translated Professor Eucken's chapter, which was one of the American addresses; to Dr. Albert C. Knudson for valuable criticism; and to Professor Eucken himself, for his generous interest and encouragement.

INTRODUCTORY

CHAPTER I

THE WORK OF BORDEN PARKER BOWNE

BY RUDOLF EUCKEN

I NEVER had the pleasure of a personal acquaintance with Dr. Bowne, and felt the touch of his personality only through our correspondence, which was, indeed, most hearty and intimate. I felt that our relation to each other was close and most friendly. He intended to visit Jena on his way to Constantinople, whither he expected to take a trip in a few months; but within a week after receiving the letter containing the news of his promised visit I received the announcement of his untimely death. It is a sad pleasure to me, and yet a satisfaction, to be able to give this evidence of my personal admiration for Dr. Bowne, and for his personality as shown in his writings.

The first general impression which one receives in taking up his books is a favorable

one, on account of the concise and definite
form in which they are written, so clear in
concept and straightforward in expression,
not at all confused or indistinct. They are
pervaded by an energy and manliness which
show no fear, either of criticism on the part
of the half-enlightened, or of the dictum of
those assuming to be in authority. On the
contrary, his words are sympathetic and almost tender in his desire to recognize what
is good in the writings of others, with an
unsparing denial of what he considers might
do harm. His works show a personal
warmth which gives the reader almost the
impression of "confessions" on the part of
a living and strong personality. This fea-
ture is especially to be valued, inasmuch as
he himself placed a very high estimate upon
personality. He says to the reader, "Above
all things be personal in the expression of
truth as you see it."

Secondly, we find in his writings his own
inmost convictions expressed clearly, and
the openness of his "confessions" is a
marked and fascinating element in them.
In reading some philosophers we feel in

them what I might call personal untruth, as in Schopenhauer, who preaches a Hindu's self-abnegation and indifference, while we find him personally the genuine epicure. The question arises at once, What have his great ideas made out of a man, if in his own life we find him to be small? On the other hand, I find in Spinoza the expression of his own inner convictions, and I must have respect for him even though I do not agree with his conclusions. In reading Bowne one respects and agrees, for there is no word uttered behind which one does not feel the man.

Let us turn now to the content of his works, the central thought. Bowne has often been placed by the side of Lotze, the famous Göttingen professor with whom he studied. There are many points of similarity as well as many differences.

First, Lotze was a logician, a dialectician; he struggled to overcome the material or else to reconcile it. Lotze's religion we feel rather to be on the fringe of life, and it is a question whether it ever affects the central thought. For this reason it does not exert any strong influence upon his philosophy. Bowne, on the contrary, puts religion at the very center, and regards it as the crown of being, maintaining that metaphysics and logic are enlightened by the fundamental question of religion, and are to be understood only in connection with it. While Bowne makes a definite distinction between religion and ethics, he makes it clear that they are inseparable, and that the one gains worth in the light of the other. The relation between them is that of the deep and underlying to its manifestation. The two should not be studied apart. And, moreover, the keynote of both lies in personality, which gives value to religion as well as to ethics. Studying them further, he maintains that religion includes ethics. This view he bases upon the close connection of religion with every kind of moral progress and advancement.

Religion cannot be proved or explained in ordinary words; neither can anything that lies deep in our nature. Aristotle asserts that the knowledge of anything must be derived from something higher than itself. Religion, therefore, would have to be proved through something of a still higher nature, and as we have access to nothing higher, it must remain unproved. Consequently, we must not try to prove it but to illustrate it; and this we may do by showing that every phenomenon depends closely upon it, and also, that an intelligent being is the established basis of every reality. Hence religion lies at the basis of our life if it is real; and if this be denied, there is nothing to fall back upon. Bowne maintains that any other attempt to explain life is due to bad thinking. The practical application of any tenet is so important in Bowne's philosophy that he takes this truth almost for granted, for by it our very life becomes exalted and valuable. The proof of religion, then, so far as it can be proved, is the creation of a new life and a new world in a man.

Secondly, the content of the world points to a unity in the universe. We must learn to see more unity in the world's phenomena, or, rather, behind them. The reign of law in all existence shows that there is interaction among all the elements of nature. What would happen if the world were made up of separate, independent particles? There would be no mutual interaction. As it is, we know that what happens in A produces a result in B, so that every phenomenon depends strictly upon a cause, and proceeds from something else. If all things were independent of one another, nothing could result. Again, this unity must rest in mind or spirit, for it is not to be found in the visible; it is to be sought in the invisible. And, once again, no spiritual mind can exist without personality, for otherwise it would be shadowy and vague and have no independent existence of its own. Such a mind must be an active, self-existent principle, and such a principle must exist; so far Lotze and Bowne advance together. Bowne further adds that this activity in nature must proceed from a God, who shall be considered the active, underlying principle. As Goethe says in Faust, "Nature is the garment of God."

There are two ways of viewing phenomena: first, as mere appearance; and, secondly, with some Being behind them as a personal Mind. Now every language has expressions for the visible, but only metaphors for the spiritual and invisible. Love is inexpressible, and cannot be defined; no more can personality. The manifestation can be described, but this has nothing to depend upon without a deeper basis for its very existence. Bowne maintained, in the face of fierce criticism, that we must be able to force our way to the certainty of some such basis. It is wrong, as well as foolish, to say that we must be content with the visible and be satisfied with leaving the invisible as something incomprehensible; and it is erroneous to say that we can appreciate only the visible. If we study the life of Luther, shall we regard him merely as a phenomenon, and say he had no real existence? No, indeed. Luther was the true man behind it all, and his acts were the expression of this hidden existence. We must believe in a creative power behind all phenomena or we are not true even to our own subjective lives.

I should like to recommend to your younger men a good subject for a dissertation, and it would be, "Bowne's Philosophy in Relation to that of Kant," together with the objections which Bowne would raise against the latter. Hegel, too, makes a great deal of "thought processes." To all this Bowne replies: "All right, if a personal existence is recognized as a basis for them; otherwise, there is no reality to these processes." Bowne is a sharp critic, not unkind, not fault-finding, but severely punishing those writers who assume to be contented with the natural, the visible, or with the impersonal spirit. He demands personal spiritual life, and consequently a living personal God, out of whom proceeds all power, and who is the active principle from whom all phenomena set forth. Another thesis that I would suggest to young men is, "Bowne as an Opponent of the Materialists," for, indeed, he was the chief opponent of naturalism. Naturalists deny the metaphysical and take the visible as the basis of their so-called metaphysics. This is illogical, as it turns effect into cause. So

Bowne criticizes evolutionists for commonly confusing the ideas of cause and effect. The visible, which is, after all, only the effect, is assumed to proceed and develop of itself. Bowne goes farther. He not only makes these truths which he asserts the basis of all real theism; he has developed a metaphysics of theism. He does not simply posit certain truths of theism, but treats all these from a metaphysical standpoint, and this is of great value to-day in the field of philosophy.

If we consider the content of religion according to Bowne and his development of it, we find three leading points which mark the chief directions of his thought: First, religion consists in life, and not in teaching or doctrine; second, the kernel of religion is ethical, and religion is the lodestar of ethics, with which it is inseparably connected; third, religion is common to all humanity. I might add as a possible definition of Bowne's standpoint that religion is the spiritual experience of humanity and is manifested in the individual.

Concerning the first point, he maintains

that religion means life, and relates to life as a whole, as well as to the whole life. In Germany certain phases of this thought have been emphasized separately, but never grasped comprehensively. With Kant religion is a moral matter, and manifested in the individual as will. For Schleiermacher it was a matter of feeling, and showed itself in the emotions; while Hegel maintained that it was a form of intelligence. These elements, which have been separated in Germany, are for Bowne only different features of one thought. He would have religion embrace all forms of life together, and he maintains that it should influence and ennoble every act and thought. Hence it is impossible to base religion on any fixed doctrine. The fundamental beliefs underlying religion from the start should be maintained, but we must allow the development from time to time of new theologies. While fundamental truths are eternal, man is still developing, and consequently these eternal truths must be manifested in the different stages of man's development in different ways.

These truths do not become new, but are newly presented. So we find in the education of children that the same truths appear to them in different lights as they grow up. True religion will change its theology, while the underlying ideas are not changeable. There has been too much abstract speculation apart from the concrete experiences of life, too much holding to abstract conceptions. Experience is the true teacher, and through her teaching we can grasp new thoughts and new views without endangering the eternal truths by abstract speculation. The old philosophy was established upon the universe as we understand it, and upon this doctrine was built up, and then life was explained according to that theory; whereas Bowne starts with life, out of which grows the world of experience, and upon this rests the doctrine, which must change as experience changes. Another good thesis would be "Bowne's Definition of Life."

James leads us back to the practical. So does Bowne, but with a different meaning, for with him, behind the practical stands the metaphysical. This is a new step in the development of philosophy. This "practical" is not that which means useful, nor that which rests upon utilitarian grounds. Still another subject for a thesis would be "The Definition of the Practical as used by Aristotle and Later Philosophers, up to Bowne." This would help to define his position. I would particularly urge the study of Bowne's philosophy, as there is always danger lest tradition, which crystallizes soon after a man's death, may put his works in a wrong light.

Bowne's contention is that the spiritual basis of life is not new, but it becomes new in its forms of development. God does not develop, but it is man that changes and develops. This is shown characteristically in the development of religious ideas; for instance, since mediæval times, when the dogmas of Catholicism were universally accepted. The study of theological development as a manifestation of religion in the varied experiences of humanity cannot but bring all views and doctrines into a clear and healthy relation to one another.

Our second point refers to the relation of
ethics to religion, upon which we have already touched. Bowne, differing from the
men of the Illumination period, as well as
from Kant, declares that religion is dis-
tinctly ethical, that ethics is the mere form
of religion. Without the latter, ethics
would have no life, content, or character, so
that ethics depends wholly upon religion.
We must not lose our bearings by a consideration of the ethical as such, but regard
it as the medium through which religion
shines and produces new life, and that the
two exert a mutual influence. So Bowne
would have us hold no harsh or crude ideas
of God's relation to the world. Theologies
of the past held that God created the world
for his own glory. This was the severe and
strict doctrine of the Jesuits, as well as of
the Calvinists. Over against this Bowne
would have us believe, with modern Christians, that he created the world out of the
fulness of his love. All religion and worship would be a form of love, and would
mean the worship of a loving Being, not of
a tyrant. The Christian should be cheerful

and joyous because his religion should make
him so. We should be glad that God
created the world and us, and that he will
save us.

The third point is one that needs em-
phasizing, particularly among Protestants,
who are apt to view religion too subjec-
tively. Bowne urges that there are many
ways of arriving at religion. There are
some that have the experience of perceiving
God's love all at once, whereupon a sudden
change comes over the man's whole nature.
Such persons are those whose temperament
is susceptible to contrasts; but this is only
one form of the manifestation of God, and
quite dependent upon the individual. There
are, on the other hand, many in whom this
change takes place more quietly. We must
only be sure of a complete turning about,
and not judge of the manner, but of the
results. Religion leads to lives, not to
theologies, for it is based upon the fundamental principles of life, and not upon
temperament or environment. In these
ideas of Bowne we find a reconciliation of
opposing views, of earnest seriousness and

happy enjoyment, of problems and con-
flicts, combined with hope and joyous
courage. We must sympathize with the
many forms of life and experience, with the
serious and the merry; and our children
should learn that they may combine the
liberty of freedom and the soberness of
earnest effort, both in their mental and in
their spiritual development.

Dr. Bowne was a philosopher of America,
and as such all America may be proud of
him and of his memory. His strong personality showed itself in such vigorous effort; his humor was so happy and flashed
forth so frequently in the midst of the
most serious work, that moroseness and
melancholy were impossible to him. He
remained fresh and youthful in spirit to the
end. Even in his last letter to me he seemed
to be more than ever pervaded with a spirit
of youth and joyous living. It is given us
to say, as did Goethe of his friend Schiller,
"He belonged to us."

CHAPTER II

THE CHANGING MOOD OF THE AGE

Dominance of the Practical in Modern Life

In a passage of the "Stones of Venice" Ruskin speaks of the high architectural beauty of the cathedral of Torcello, built by the Venetians as they took refuge from their pursuers, on the half submerged sand dunes of the Adriatic. He says, "The actual condition of the exiles who built the cathedral of Torcello is exactly typical of the spiritual condition which every Christian ought to recognize in himself, a state of homelessness on earth, except so far as he can make the Most High his habitation."[1]

A more recent writer, speaking of the present age, has said: "When man was doubtful if he would see to-morrow's sun-

[1] Stones of Venice, vol. ii. p. 13.

rise, he built as if not dreaming of a perishable home. To-day, when he cannot believe that death will touch him, and his orderly life stretches forward as an endless end of the world, he will leave for the amazement of future ages the Crystal Palace and the City Temple and the Peabody Building."[2]

These descriptions present by vivid contrast the material basis of the changing mood of the age. Whatever men build, whether it be of brick and stone, institutions of government and civilization, or systems of thought and education, the sense of dependence upon the Eternal, the attitude toward the things not seen, will inevitably write itself into all their work.

The outward and material circumstances of man's position on the earth will reflect themselves in his philosophy and dictate the mood of his thought. The age of grinding poverty, of elemental struggle toward freedom and knowledge, is always an age of faith and optimism. The age of material fullness, when man seems to have almost within his grasp the secrets of the universe,

---

[2] Masterman, In Peril of Change, p. 170.

the ultimate triumph over poverty, ignorance, and the brute forces of nature, is the age when pessimism and despair range deepest. The human spirit is so constituted that when man must take up an heroic struggle, in which life and the most precious interests are daily put in jeopardy, his dreams and faiths exalt him to the skies. When these material things and the external forms for which he fought seem forever assured, he is plunged into doubt and morbid self-examination by his unsatisfied soul.

To understand the philosophical mood of our own age it is necessary to keep in mind the dominating elements in our material progress. The prevalence of scientific investigation and the growth of the scientific spirit have given us a hitherto unknown environment for our thought. With the mastery of physical forces the old horror of nature has passed. With it has gone a great deal that was merely tradition, prejudice, and superstition. Beyond the borders of childhood we live in no magic world. Laws of nature are to us as an open book and in many minds the only book possessing any authority. Even the common man feels that he has deciphered, or will have deciphered for him in the near future, the last of nature's secrets. There is to be nothing left at which to wonder. We are amazed no longer at the vastness of the universe, at its marvelously interlocking processes, or at its hints of Final Purpose; but, rather, at ourselves that we know so much. In the spirit of Goldsmith's lines, we can say of man that

> Still the wonder grows
> That one small head can carry all he knows.

The most startling discoveries in nature provoke but a momentary enthusiasm. We are masters of nature.

With the passing of the old feeling toward nature has come a new acquaintance among the peoples of the earth. Nothing is perhaps more startling than the adoption by pagan and strange bloods of modern inventions, the latest philosophies and schemes of education. That which has been the product of generations of struggle is suddenly appropriated by men of other races and civilizations. We are chagrined at the ease and adaptability at our own game of genius and invention of these strange and long-despised peoples. Whether we wish it or not, they represent mighty forces to be reckoned with. The overcoming of space and time sets them in our own dooryard. Tokyo, Peking, and Calcutta are nearer than London, Paris, and New York were yesterday. We are reminded of their thought in every review, of their deeds in the morning paper, and we eat of their products at every breakfast table. A new world of human relationships has dawned upon us, in which we are burdened with a responsibility which we cannot escape.

The resources of science have been put at the service of the industrial world. The discoveries of the past generation have revolutionized the world of commerce and labor. The comforts and luxuries of life have vastly increased. Great fortunes have resulted, and with them an overwhelming eagerness to discover the sesame of wealth. The contribution of science to this new world of material things has elevated scientific dogma into unquestioned power. The gravest criticism and deepest slur, that according to the average man can be cast, is the criticism and the slur of being unscientific. Little room is left for the æsthetic, the idealistic, or the spiritual. To such an age it has seemed, speaking in the words of Noyes's "Resurrection," that

Love was too small, too human to be found
   In that transcendent source whence love was
      born;
We talked of "forces": heaven was crowned
   With philosophic thorn.

The demands made upon all departments of life have thus become intensely practical and utilitarian. What does it accomplish? How great are the returns? These are the questions that are constantly asked, not only in the world of economics, but also in the worlds of philosophy and religion. The demand of pragmatism is the demand of the modern spirit elevated into a test for truth. And this demand is not without its basis of sanity and justice. Men are wearied of theories and systems which appear divorced from every practical interest. But too often the pragmatic question is made so individualistic and so fragmentary that truth becomes a mere utility for the moment and occasion only.

To all of this is added the feeling that in our fullness and material prosperity we have no need to be comforted either by philosophy or religion. The former contents itself too largely with the explanation of the material, and the latter approaches an unredeemed world with a timidity that leaves no place for authoritative appeal. The indecision and blindness of a great multitude is voiced in Swinburne's "Watch in the Night":

> I halt and hearken behind
> If haply the hours will go back
> And return to the dear dead light,
> To the watch fires and stars that of old
> Shone where the sky now is black.

THE STRUGGLE FOR UNITY

The main streams of philosophic thought, materialism, and idealism have run their

course, and neither has been able to bring
philosophic peace, except in the minds of
their most extreme partisans. To the
former has been given the popular role by
reason of her close allegiance with practical
science, and the inability of the average
man to sense the problems that hedge her
way. To common sense, all the ways of
materialism are pleasantness, and all her
paths are peace. The world is just what it
appears to be. Material atoms are con-
jured up to impinge upon nerves; and
mind, thought, and purpose are the easy
result of mechanical forces. Memory follows the grooves plowed in the brain by
yesterday's experience, while other memories await the expectant call, filed carefully
away, according to the best modern business
methods, in their appropriate pigeonholes.
When all is so easily imagined, he would
seem to be only a fool who would question.
In this system nothing is denied the imagination and only the facts are wanting.
On such a theory everything becomes as
sun-clear, from the first accidental jiggling
of atoms to the philosopher at the other end

of the line, as the continuous juvenile tragedy of The House that Jack Built. Unfortunately for the comfort of materialism, the barrenness of the supposed solution is coming to the attention of her own disciples, and we have the old garment patched with the new cloth of pragmatism and Creative Evolutions. These reach the solemn decision that "universe" is a term of delusion and must yield to pluralism or at least to dualism.

Nor has professional idealism been more fortunate in the endeavor to unite the sundered sides of consciousness. The world of materialism has been one in which matter was all and spirit nothing, but the world of idealism has been one in which the reality of matter has been altogether denied. She has been no more able to command men with authority than has her opponent. The material world bulks so large in the common experience that it is ever difficult to convince men that

> The solid earth, the round sun,
> And all the visible world of sight and sound,
> Are but the phantasmagoria of a dream.

Thus the ancient battle between materialism and idealism has raged since the days of the Greek philosophers, and not until our own generation have the conflicting arguments been sufficiently sifted and analyzed to show that neither bald materialism nor absolute idealism can present a possible solution to the enigma of the universe.

THE PRESENT CRISIS

We have to-day the natural successors of idealism, who cling to the thought of unity, thrust out by time and criticism from the ancient peace of an absolutism whose only ultimate reality is the divine Spirit, hard pressed to answer the problem of evil. If all we see is the manifestation of the Divine, whence comes evil in the world? This is the insistent question cast at the spokesmen of idealism. Thinking men are impatient of any denial of the reality of pain, evil, or sorrow, in an effort to save the character of God. The sense of suffering and injustice is more acute than ever in the history of the world. A God that will

41

cause suffering, pain, and evil they will repudiate. Even that human being seems a monster who will not do his best to alleviate misery of every sort. How much more will they despise a Supreme Being so obtuse to moral responsibility as to create men for pain! The supreme question of the age for idealism as well as for Theism is how to maintain a Moral Causal Intelligence in the face of existent evil and suffering.

It might be thought that, in view of these conditions, the way of the materialists would be easy. A cursory examination will show, however, that it is no longer possible for materialism to imagine that she speaks in terms of universe. Even the most obtuse materialist is to-day forced to admit a power and a reality, which, whether he knows or not, is not provided for in his system. He has before him the expedient of a dualism somewhat after the fashion of Mr. Bergson's, or he may resort with Mr. James to a pluralistic world. But such a universe falls more and more, the farther we search, into a disjointed and ever-dissolving individualism in which all realities disappear at the touch like Apples of Sodom. The lack of order and purpose is mistaken for freedom, and much dilated upon. The tumbrils daily cart the Theists to the slaughter in the interests of the new-found emancipation, and there is not missing the grim joy of the populace at the effectiveness of the guillotine of freedom. Still there is ever present at the feast of joy a lurking Banquo's ghost of Purposive Intelligence that refuses to keep decently buried; the Great Perhaps, for which the heart of man cries out like a lonely child in the night.

> Just when we're safest there's a sunset touch,
> A fancy from a flower-bell, some one's death,
> A chorus-ending from Euripides—
> And that's enough for fifty hopes and fears
> As old and new at once as nature's self
> To rap and knock and enter in our soul.

THE NEW TASK OF PHILOSOPHY

The new task of philosophy is the reconciliation of these contrasting views. Much critical work has already been done which makes repetition unnecessary. There is a generally clear recognition of the real issues at stake. The individual mood toward one or the other side will greatly influence the result in any particular case, but yet there is reason to hope that we can come to an understanding of the issues involved, if we cannot unite in a common explanation. It is true that the old, old questions of the nature of reality, of Creative Purpose and evil, of unity or diversity, of freedom or necessity, will remain; but in the coming age we shall approach them from a new angle and see them in a new light. While we cannot expect to settle them, we may hope to work toward a solution. We may find a standpoint from which life may go on without despair or the eclipse of faith in the things of the spirit.

In the realization of this new task of philosophy we believe that the future will have to reckon with the work of one of our foremost philosophers whom Rudolf Eucken is pleased to call a "world philosopher." His purpose was to show how the contrasting and apparently irreconcilable questions might find solution and common ground in the recognition of personality. Eucken declares that "we need something eternal to bind the different ages together, but this eternal has grown dim amid our doubts and struggles."[3] This is true for history and for individual thought as well. This need Bowne would meet with his doctrine of personalism. To show the implications of this theory with relation to the different phases of thought is the purpose of this volume.

Because we believe that the case for faith has not been closed, nor its last word spoken, we come to the task in the mood of Swinburne's lines:

> The tides and the hours run out,
> And the seasons of death and of doubt,
> The night watches bitter and sore.

Even the clamors and confusions of warring peoples will confirm the prophecy of our Lord, and be but the birth-pangs of a better world. The night ebbs away and across the hills lies the dawn.

---

[3] Christianity and the New Idealism, p. 38.

SECTION I
NATURALISM

CHAPTER III

THE MODERN SPELL OF A GREEK PHANTOM

THE ANCIENT DREAM OF MATERIAL UNITY

WHATEVER it may imply, the human mind has ever shown a remarkable thirst to achieve unity. The apparent relationships in a world of great diversity make possible the belief that all things proceed from the same source. The world of things is assumed to be a universe and the mind of man has never been able permanently to rest in any other assumption. Unity is sought, whether in a material protoplasm from which all things have developed, or in a final ground of divine Thought or Purpose. Between the two ideas the philosophical world has been divided from early times into the opposing camps of material-

ism and idealism. The search of the early
Greek school was for this primal essence of
things. Certain conclusions then reached
have exerted an overwhelming influence in
the scientific thought of our own age. It
is interesting to glance at the movement in
its beginnings. The great contribution of
Greek philosophy to modern science was
the theory that the material world is made
up of atoms. With Leucippus, the founder
of the theory, the atoms were countless,
infinite in variety, imperceptibly small, having only the quality of filling space. They
were in motion from eternity, and so held
within them all the possibilities of pro-
ducing the visible world. The importance
of this theory for science lay in the fact
that all qualitative differences could be accounted for by varying the quantities and
combination of atoms.

To the thoughtful it is at once apparent
that with the materialist the atom is endowed with that magic and with those
undiscoverable powers which the idealist
ascribes to a World-Soul, or Divine Intelligence. In the case of the materialist the

unaccountable powers of the fabled atom
are overlooked in the beginning because
they seem insignificant, yet when some real
explanation is needed they are marshaled
in such masses as to become suddenly
visible, and sufficient to account for any
result. Of course what has actually taken
place is a flight of the imagination. Whether
it has represented truly the order of nature
we are left in confused doubt if we be un-
imaginative souls.

Protagoras added to the atomism of
Leucippus the further doctrine that perception itself rests upon the motion of
atoms, and that perceiving and thinking
are psychologically identical. All perceptions that come to us are true for us, just
as they appear. Hence the famous maxim
loved by the modern Humanist, "Man is
the measure of all." Perceptions, under
this scheme, are only relatively true. There
can be no universal standard of truth.
However, it must be noted that in this
system perception is something other than
the perceiving subject, and is likewise something apart from the object perceived. This

discrepancy, though apparent, remains un-answered. So soon in our search for ma-terialistic unity have we happened on a divided world.

THE PHANTOM OF FORM AND SPACE

With Democritus, the system of material-ism is at last in full flower. Observing the relativity of Protagoras' scheme of percep-tion, Democritus transcends it to assert the possibility of knowledge of the real through thought. Both Democritus and Plato were in this sense rationalistic, but Plato's ra-tionalism took an ethical turn. He sought the knowledge of the true Being as a means to virtue. His philosophy grew out of ethical need. With Plato perception ap-plies only to the corporeal world and can give opinions only. Thought, on the other hand, leads us to a higher and ultimate truth and knowledge of the True Being.

Democritus kept to the way of material-ism. "Pure Form," with Plato, had been a general term corresponding to logical spe-cies, but Democritus meant by this term atom forms. To the motion of atoms he refers perception and all mental activities whatsoever. The mind, or soul, or whatever may be named as the perceiving subject, consists of atoms which differ from other atoms only in fineness, as the atoms of fire were said to be finer than those of other substances. In a perceiving being the fire atoms were assumed to exist in about the proportion of one in three. By this simple and easy speculation was laid the basis of later materialism with its knowing and purposive monads, corpuscular attractions and repulsions, atomic loves and hates, vital sparks and *elans vitaux*, which at least to the advocates of the system are sufficient to account for the world and all that dwell therein. "Thus the prejudice in favor of what may be perceived or imaged (*anschaulich*), as if spatial form and motion were something simpler, more comprehensible in themselves, and less of a problem than qualitative character and alteration, is made the principle for the theoretical explanation of the world."[1]

---

[1] Windelband, History of Philosophy, p. 111.

PERSONALISM AND THE

The theories of Democritus passed on through the Epicureans in so far as they involved atomism and mechanism. But Epicurus was weak in his conception of the necessary causation of mechanical forces. He differed from Democritus in denying altogether the existence of purpose in matter. He held that the causeless deviation of atoms was sufficient to explain the worlds. Such a statement of the doctrine would have been of little use to the scientific age that was coming, but fortunately the Stoics preserved that which the Epicureans lacked of Democritus' doctrine. Through their pantheistic conception of the Deity as the "vital principle" they arrived at belief in an absolute causal necessity. Thus they continued that which the Epicureans had lost in the shuffle—the idea of a universal reign of law.[2]

When at last the long reign of Neoplatonism and scholasticism was ended by the shock of discovery and renaissance, it was

2 Sc. Windelband, History of Philosophy, p. 183.

the complementary ideas of mechanical causation and reign of law that proved so potent to the new generation of scientific investigators.

REVIVAL AND DEVELOPMENT OF THE DOCTRINE IN MODERN SCIENCE

The tool had been preserved, and was ready when the syllogistic form of reasoning introduced by Aristotle had spent its force and had shown its inadequacy to deal singlehanded with practical problems. The world had grown tired of the weary round of dialectic. The reaction was for that reason all the more intense. But the tool was yet to be perfected.

Bruno led the way by his conception of the monad, which in truly Hylozoistic fashion he endowed with potentiality. He affirmed the homogeneity of the universe, and declared that all qualitative determinations must be traced to quantitative changes.

Bacon, casting off the rigors of scholastic method, declared that induction from particular experiences is the only true method of science.

Galileo contributed an insistence upon the application of the mathematical principle to scientific investigation, with this difference: instead of applying it to Being he applied it to Becoming, or change. Thus with his brilliant contemporaries he laid the foundations for modern astronomy.

Descartes made a contribution of greatest importance in that while he insisted on the certainty afforded by induction, he also demanded that the principle thus attained should by the method of composition afford explanation to the whole round of experience.

THE DIFFICULTY OF NATURALISTIC EXPLANATION

Why, then, should we remain unsatisfied with a principle which in the material world has so proved its practical worth? Why should Greek atomism, lying at the basis of the modern discovery of nature, receive the unworthy title of "phantom"? For this reason: while it has furnished an invaluable method of procedure in investigation, its leading postulates are yet unproved. Many of them remain as much in the realm of the imagination as they did in the crude theories of the sixth century before Christ. The weakness of the supporters of naturalism has in the main been their inability to recognize the possible truth and value of the theory for physics, without reviving the ghost of ancient speculation and insisting that it has equal force for metaphysics.

Whatever the attempt of materialism to explain life and mind, whether through the Hylozoistic endowment of atoms with sense or the hiding of the fact of self-directing personality under the verbiage of "states of consciousness," it can do no more than explain half the world. For the thinking mind, burdened with the explanation of its own consciousness and volition, seeking to know its rightful place in the universe and to understand itself, the half world explained by naturalism is the half that is least important. It needs ever to be kept in mind that knowledge of the laws of change, of precedence and sequence, while giving us sure ground on which to build our human expectations, tells us nothing of the essence of that which acts. As a method of science atomism is to be judged solely by its value as a guide upon the road, not to metaphysical explanation, but to the human mastery of physical forces. It is good so long as it proves valuable, and only to that extent.

Perhaps the most humorous thing in the history of philosophy—if humor can ever be said to invade so dreary a realm—is the attempt of naturalism to account for thought and will, decrying the vagueness and abstraction of the idealist, and at the same moment introducing into its conception of the atom the illusory, magical, and abstract powers which it condemns in the God of its opponents. One inevitably reverts to the picture of Faust traveling the Pharsalian fields in the Walpurgis Night, with Homonculus speaking to him out of a bottle. The materialist may prefer a God whose magic powers can all be confined in a test tube, but there will always remain some who cannot discover folly in believing in a God both immanent and transcendent, after the manner of Sidney Lanier, "My God is great, my God is strong."

58

CHAPTER IV

THE EVADED PROBLEMS OF SPENCER'S PHILOSOPHY

It would seem unnecessary to take much space for examination of the now generally discredited system of Herbert Spencer. Because he was the spokesman for the naturalistic school; because he long held sway over the popular mind as the representative of scientific thinking; and because it was Bowne who early called attention to the metaphysical inconsistencies of his position, we enter here upon a brief discussion of his work.

The naturalistic school itself now sees the untenability of Spencer's favorite positions. By no one of any school has he been more sharply arraigned than by Mr. Bergson. But this arraignment comes forty years after the clean-cut criticisms of the young Bowne. Bowne's criticisms were offered at a time when the empirical philosophy was both in physics and metaphysics in the ascendant. It was then an unpopular thing to venture criticism. Forgiveness was never accorded him in the minds of some for his sacrilegious daring in the presence of this idol of their thought. To take an attitude of criticism seemed at the time opposed to all that judgment and right sense science and reality dictated. The possession of clearer ideas by the philosophical world to-day upon the proper limits of scientific investigation is doubtless in some measure due to the pitiless criticism and constructive thought of Bowne.

THE MUCH-KNOWN UNKNOWABLE

One secret of Spencer's popularity lay in his apparent reconciliation of science and religion in a time of intense bitterness. He was essentially monistic, and yet, while yielding the claims of empirical science, seemed to leave place for a Divine Creative Power. It is true that he left to the religious a poor sort of God, but at the moment they were glad to be left anything.

Spencer repudiated with warmth the charge of being a materialist and strove to keep his thought free from it. Nevertheless, the logic of his doctrine of mind inevitably landed him there, though unwilling and protesting.

The loophole by which he hoped to admit the Divine Being, and so save the cause of religion, is the very one through which the Purposive Intelligence is compelled to make his escape from the system. To admit God at all was to make him so vaguely indefinite as not to be able to interfere with the natural world. Relieved of this responsibility, there was nothing left that was of any consequence to our thought of the Divine.

Spencer declared for the phenomena of experience as the only source of knowledge. When we go back of these we hit at once upon the absolute, are lost in an infinite regress, and are told that the absolute can never be a cause. Concerning this absolute we can make no affirmation, and, therefore, he applies to it the term "Unknowable." Thus he seems at first to be determined to confine himself to the actions and interactions of the phenomenal world, and science and religion seem placed on an equal footing regarding the Unknowable. As soon, however, as religion has been consigned to the region of pure mystery we discover a strange and unaccountable activity in the Unknowable. We were told to reject religious assumptions regarding the Unknowable because they involved an infinitude of time, which was unthinkable. Once we are well freed from the religious realm, however, we are no longer to be constrained by such considerations. We begin to be able to affirm many things of the Unknowable. In the words of John Stuart Mill, which Bowne was fond of quoting, we begin to possess "a prodigious amount of knowledge concerning the Unknowable." We find that it is omnipresent in time and space; that it is related to the system of experience; "Coexistences and sequences in experience point to coexistences and sequences in the fundamental reality." We learn that the Unknowable is subject to time and change; that it is one, eternal, power, reality, the cause of phenomena, persistent, and indestructible, "The infinite and eternal energy on which all things depend and from which all things forever proceed." Though we have not been allowed to affirm anything of the Unknowable for religious faith, yet such affirmation becomes the mainstay of the system of physics. In the religious realm we were ordered to reject all conclusions requiring an infinitude of time, but in the physical realm we are commanded to invoke such an infinitude in order to account for the system. We are to pass to this by affirming an indestructibility of matter, and an ever-persistent force, which, indeed, phenomena will not enable us to prove, but which we must imagine.

It is true that Spencer tries to save the absolute, after having banished it from his kingdom, by saying that we have an indefinite consciousness of it. Examination shows that an indefinite consciousness is worth nothing for any practical purpose, is nothing more than a form of words. We feel again as Wordsworth expressed himself:

> I'd rather be
> A pagan suckled in a creed outworn;
> So might I, standing on this pleasant lee,
> Have glimpses that would make me less forlorn.

THE LITTLE-KNOWN REALITY

A similar negativing indefiniteness attends Spencer's account of reality. We have seen how unsafe and improper he considers it to affirm anything like personality or purpose of the Unknowable. Inasmuch as the fundamental reality bulks back on the Unknowable, we can affirm nothing except certain coexistences and sequences which are witnessed in phenomena. All knowledge is thus made relative to the individual who perceives in any given case. There is, indeed, no power assigned by which the individual can recognize similarity in phenomena, or reason from individual experiences to general laws. Memory is unaccounted for because no personality is provided to relate "faint states of consciousness." Dependent, as we are, upon an Unknowable of which we can affirm nothing, it is difficult to see how we can be certain at all that there is a world of things corresponding to our perceptions.

At this point he meets, according to Bowne, with a double problem. He is forced to rescue science from the skeptical conclusions of his know-nothing argument. At the same time he is compelled to state a doctrine of phenomena and of knowledge which will provide a foundation for science and save his system from materialism and atheism. To escape agnosticism he calls back the cashiered and discredited notions of matter, force, motion, time, and space, treating them as if there had never been any doubt of their standing and making them the foundation on which to build.

The other half of the problem he meets by asserting the relative nature of reality, defining it as "persistence in consciousness." Reality is, then, the effect produced in us by the fundamental reality, or the Unknowable. In this case Bowne raises a question. Would the Unknowable be able to do anything in our absence? If so, then these relative realities are something more than effects in us, and the definition is inadequate. If the relative realities do not exist in our absence, then reality is a mere subjectivity, as illusive as a dream.

Spencer makes his final appeal to the claims of the persistence of force and the indestructibility of matter. By persistence of force he declares himself to mean "the persistence of some cause that transcends our knowledge and conception." Thus we are brought back as a last resort to the much-known Unknowable about which we can affirm nothing. The assumed law of the indestructibility of matter would seem likewise insufficient as a basis for a doctrine of phenomena. It may be sufficiently accurate as a working basis in the physical realm, but it cannot be accurately demonstrated even there. In the case of the wedge or the lever we determine the exact amount of power, resistance, friction, and heat, and on paper write an equation which is sufficiently correct for practical purposes. But, speaking with the exactitude required by a law of indestructibility, there are losses in the process that we cannot compute nor include. Our equation is an approximation of the fact. We speak of the transmutation of friction, weight of falling water, or energy of steam into electrical power, light, or heat, and can come sufficiently near for practical purposes, but along the way much has to go unaccounted for. We cannot turn the processes backward and get the first terms of our equation. In other words, science can secure a practical working basis after the law of indestructibility. It cannot do more.

In the end we find that Spencer cannot meet his problem without assuming for his persistence of force and indestructibility of matter that very infinitude of time against which he has warned us in the religious realm. He cannot prove these laws in any given case, but he can imagine that they might be true if they were given an infinite time in which to work.

THE THEORY OF EVOLUTION

Spencer's theory of evolution, though not originating with him, and advanced first in the early Greek philosophy, was the part of his system which gave him the widest reading and popularity. In his statement of the theory we find much philosophical unsoundness.

The main support of his definition of evolution lies in his dependence upon the fallacy of the universal. This is the fallacy which vitiates general statements and makes for half-truths. It is a part of the busy-body's statement, "Every one is saying," when the exact truth is that the busybody is saying. If we can multiply atoms sufficiently to make impossible the tracing of any individual atom, and can multiply to an indefinite length the time in which they have to work, we can observe without wonder any imagined result. The point at issue is further lost in the words with which Spencer covers up the gap from the inorganic to the organic, from organic to sentient, from sentient to reasoning being. This is done by employing a word in slightly different senses, and so the gulf is bridged, linguistically speaking. But never yet hath eye seen nor ear heard how or when one single atom was led across the gulf to become a living soul.

Moreover, if we are compelled to assume with Spencer the logical equivalence of cause and effect, the definition has no meaning. If I must say of any effect that all of its elements were already contained in its cause, the passing from one to the other is no progress. It cannot explain the elements of novelty which enter in. It would certainly be inadequate to explain the emergence of the present world from the original dance of atoms. Mr. Bergson has directed his sharpest shafts at this conception of evolution. He compares it to putting together a puzzle picture, all the parts of which have been previously fitted and prepared, and then with childish imagination assuming that a creative progress has been made.

THE DEFINITION OF LIFE AND MIND

It is Spencer's doctrine of mind that exposes the materialistic trend of his philosophy. Judged from his doctrine of matter, Spencer rightly claimed not to be a materialist. Judged from his doctrine of mind, materialism was his inevitable goal.

According to the statement of the evolution formula, life is to be defined in terms of matter and motion. These in turn are but the symbols of the Unknowable. Here Bowne calls attention to the fact that the atoms may be chemically regrouped, and can also be summoned forth in sufficient numbers to cause considerable masses. Bowne asks, however, what chemical distribution can be made which will be more than a distribution or combination of chemicals. So long as it is a chemical combination it can be resolved into its constituent elements. Borrowing a word from the biological realm to cover the discrepancy between chemical atom and living protoplasm is not an actual but a verbal process. We are not told how matter or motion becomes something essentially different—that is, a living organism.

In like manner, in his theory of mind Spencer is satisfied with bridging verbally the gap between an affection of the nerves and a consciousness of the external world. He does this by asserting a double face to all nervous action. But it is useless to talk of a double-faced character for nervous action. We would still be bound to explain how an affection of the auditory nerve can be more than pleasurable or painful, soft or harsh, faint or vivid. Whence comes the mental content? There must be something more than the affection of a nerve, or I should not recognize the voice I hear as my mother's, to say nothing of the attendant thought and memory which stir into consciousness all the springs of loyalty and affection. How shall I judge whether a sharp affection of my nerves is the "Soldier's Chorus" or a toothache? The "face" of nervous action by which I come to knowledge tells me nothing about the other "face" at all, but speaks directly of that outside world which impinges upon consciousness. If I say the effects produced in me are only the attendants upon certain nervous affections, I have yet to show how I can consider my consciousness a true picture of what I seem to see. I must further explain how in this system of fleeting experiences, the factors of experience are by good fortune related each to each, or how the memory of yesterday can persist with any real meaning for to-day.

We are shut up to a world of nervous action. The structure that we build thereon is without common validity or verification. With or against our wills, if we cling to Spencer's system, we come to haven in a universe purely materialistic, from which even the Unknowable is powerless to save us.

CHAPTER V

BOWNE AS AN ANTAGONIST OF NATURALISM

ALL PHILOSOPHICAL VALUES HINGE ON THE DEFINITION OF REALITY

THE real import of any system of thought eventually rests with its doctrine of reality. In regard to the nature of reality we have noted the two great antagonistic streams of thought. Under the first category are included those thinkers who assume matter as the basal reality. It makes little difference whether they proceed upon the theory of magical and metaphysical atoms endowed with energy, motion, and force, or whether they conceal the metaphysical drift of their arguments by the assumption of vital impulses, reactions, affinities, selection, or what not. In the end the sufficiency of all such theories will be found to lie in the ignoring of a part of the problem. Disaster is avoided only by refusal to carry the

problem to its logical conclusion. Such is
the end of all materialism.

Plato attempted to meet the tide of materialistic thought by raising the barrier of
ideal knowledge. To him the universal was
the true reality. The universally true was
forever beyond the cavil or denial of individuals. He thus erected in thought an
idealism that through Neoplatonism profoundly influenced Christian theology for
centuries.

Aristotle, his pupil, noted the impassable
gulf in Plato's world between the ideal and
the actual and attempted to bridge it. He
declared that reality could not exist as a
general term, but must be found in concrete and particular instances. As Aristotle
labored to bring together the universal and
the particular, and to let the Platonic
idealism down to earth, so Bowne aimed to
join the sundered sides of philosophic
thought. Knowing the importance of the
doctrine of reality to the future implications of his system, he stated his definition
with unusual care. Reality with Bowne was
active and causal, that which can act or be

acted upon. He thus made possible the assumption of the reality of thought without falling prey to the phenomenalism of the absolute idealist.

The naturalist, by assuming an atomic causation for all mental perception, invests each idea, right or wrong, with fundamental validity. He leaves no room, either, for the substantiation of mental possessions that come by the way of reflection. He is not only faced by the problem of error; he is at loss to account for all reflective knowledge.

From the opposite direction, the absolute idealist encounters difficulty with the problem of evil. If thought in man is simply a reflection of God's thought, the burden of all evil and malicious thinking, error, superstition, and baseless fears is laid upon the Infinite Mind.

Now if, as with Bowne, the essence of reality is simply causal activity, no such difficulties arise. The world of things depends upon the causal activity of a Divine Personality. The mutual relations and interactions of the world spring from the unity of the Supreme Will. The mind of man grasps a true world because both thinker and thing are included in the one creative harmony. We have an inkling of how this may be in the causal efficiency of the human personality, which is able to penetrate matter and to make matter conform to it. This may, indeed, be a great mystery to the materialist, but it is a truth which no man can doubt without the overthrow of confidence in the reality of his own experience.

It might seem that while Bowne has by this process escaped the problem of error, he has not been so fortunate with the problem of evil. And yet the problem of evil, that crux of theism, as the problem of error is the nightmare of materialism, ceases to maintain so great a tyranny. Dr. Bowne would have been far from claiming for his system the solution of the problem. But under the order of Personalism evil is no longer the necessary expression of the fundamental reality, nor is it loaded upon the Divine Will. It is, rather, an attendant upon the granting of freedom to responsible human personalities, it being more dear to the Divine to secure moral character than to create an otherwise perfect but morally irresponsible world. It is at least thinkable that to a God of moral capacity an unmoral world would be imperfect. If at the end of long disciplines he can bring mankind up to a moral perfection that is true because voluntary, might that not be the perfect world that should satisfy the divine thought? This mingling of human and divine personality and purpose has been thus beautifully expressed by Alfred Noyes in his poem "Creation":

When he is older he shall be
    My friend and walk here at My side
Or—when he wills—grow young with Me,
    And, to that happy world where once We died,
Descending through the calm, blue weather,
    Buy life once more with our immortal breath,
And wander through the little fields together,
    And taste of Love and Death.

Is God Immanent Mover or Prime Mover?

Naturalism can secure nothing more than a phenomenal world. If the stirring of atoms gives us perception, and chemical or molecular change in the cells of the brain is alone responsible for ideas, we are still at loss to explain how molecular changes can give us thought and a knowledge of the world of relations. What we really have is an affection of the nerves. When we attempt to reason from these nervous affections to a world of relations we have no reason to assume that we have more than phenomena. We have no means of proving our world to be a real one. The reason is that moving from the materialistic standpoint we have not assumed a ground sufficiently inclusive to take in the thinker and the thing.

We are at an equal loss on the naturalistic plane to trace effects to a first cause. We cannot follow the series far until we discover that we are involved in an infinite regress. Each effect demands a preceding cause. The earliest cause becomes more troublesome for explanation than the latest. In despair we may be led to affirm with Spencer that the first cause is the Unknowable. Then we are compelled to face the question of how the knowable can spring from the unknowable. Aristotle attempted to solve this deadlock by positing a Divine Will as the Prime Mover.[1] Such a world would find its unity in a primal impulse, but would fall victim to a doctrine of necessity only less rigid than that of naturalism. Bowne meets this problem by assuming that the fundamental causal activity is not a Prime Mover, but an Immanent Mover continually manifesting himself in the on-going of the world. Such a conception does not conflict with the laws of natural science, for Bowne draws a careful distinction between phenomenal and efficient causality. Natural science is built upon the laws of sequence in phenomena. We can affirm the order in which events will occur without making any metaphysical assumptions at all. The efficient cause of the action and interaction of the natural order is the Divine Personality establishing his own laws of procedure.

THE PERSONALITY OF THE WORLD-GROUND

At this point we find Bowne going beyond the thought of Aristotle to affirm personal-

---

[1] Aristotle, Metaphysics, Book xi, chap. vii.

ity in the Divine Being. This thought would have been repugnant to Aristotle, but his failure to affirm it made impossible the maintenance of a moral order and of personal immortality. This fact is most clearly brought out by Eucken. He says: "Aristotle affirms the existence of a transcendent Deity as the source of reason, and as the origin of motion, which from eternity to eternity pervades the universe. But he denies to this Deity any activity within the world; concern with external things, not to say petty human affairs, would destroy the completeness of the Deity's life. So God, or pure intelligence, himself unmoved, moves the world by his mere being; any further development of things arises from their own nature. Here, accordingly, there is no moral order of the world, and no Providence. Likewise there can be no hope of a personal immortality.'

In contrast with Aristotle, Bowne declares that "Causal explanation must be in terms of personality or it must vanish altogether." This view is strictly in accord

[2] The Problem of Human Life, p. 47.

with all that we know of causation. Prece-
dences and sequences in phenomena could
give to individual atoms no knowledge of
the meaning of the processes of which they
are a part. Phenomenal causes would be
confined to the effects which they themselves produced, and in any case we would
be forced to an infinite regress. In human
personality alone we have introduced into
experience of causation that which is an
uncaused cause of phenomena. The human
personality, being able to relate a succession
of causes and effects to itself, and standing
outside the mechanical circle, becomes measurably an efficient cause. But the human
personality in order to preserve the in-
tegrity of its own thought bulks back on an
eternal thinking Personality through which
it finds its synthesis with the world of
things and persons. Thus the human personality, introducing an unaccounted factor
into the realm of nature, gives a hint of the
place of the Divine Personality in this
order. If this uncaused and purposive personal element be left out, we can have no
efficient causation and no real progress. On

the impersonal plane the effect must be already contained in the cause, and there can be no progress. To say that the effect is only potentially contained in the cause is to introduce the new factor surreptitiously under the cover of a word. Any World-Ground capable of real causation, not itself involved in the atomic flux, must be personal as well as intelligent.

Is Freedom Possible in the Natural World?

As has already been pointed out, any system of mechanical explanation falls inevitably into difficulty with the problem of evil, as well as with the problem of error. If all thinking and action is caused by atomic motion, then we are bound to a system of necessity, and moral action becomes impossible. The criminal in his crime is then simply fulfilling the necessary result of affections of his nerves. He is much to be pitied, but not at all to be blamed. Every sort of error and extravagance is given an equal footing with truth and sanity. Only a little reflection serves to show how deeply this theory would cut into every demand of the moral order.

By positing all causal efficiency as arising from personality, place is left for the existence of error and evil without offending the human sense of moral obligation or erecting error into the plane of truth, or of burdening the Deity with responsibility for evil. It is impossible to explain the problem of evil in any general way that will give satisfaction, because man is a moral being and so constituted that the existence of evil is forever an offense; and because, further, the problem can be met only on the arena of action and solved only in the individual life. It is possible to hold such a view as not to offend the most treasured instincts of the heart. This Bowne has done by reason of his definition of reality and by the assumption of personality in the World-Ground.

SECTION II
IDEALISM

CHAPTER VI

THE KANTIAN STARTING-POINT

Has the Mind a Task in Experience?

Kant's great contribution to the world of thought was his discovery that the mind has a task in experience. He affirmed truly when he declared that his work would make as great a change in the outlook of philosophy as had the discoveries of Copernicus in the field of astronomy.

Hitherto the mind had been regarded as the passive recipient of impressions, a tablet on which the world of external things could write itself. Kant showed that every experience was due to the constitutive activity of the mind itself, as well as to the impressions of the outside world. Time and space had been conceived as fundamental realities which could exist apart from all intelligence. He aimed to show how they were but the forms under which the thinking mind relates the world of things and events to itself and to each other. This power of the mind to bring a real contribution of its own to experience will be apparent if we consider how the world of nature yields a decidedly richer content to the biologist than to the man ignorant of her processes. She speaks to the trained mind a thousand things unnoticed by the untrained, and every addition to the mental capital increases the synthesizing power of the beholder.

That space is a necessary form of thinking, an intuition rather than an acquirement of experience, is to be illustrated in many ways. In dreams, though there is no actual space, the mind works under the space form. In traveling distances during the unconsciousness of sleep, and even for places never seen, the mind proceeds to construct ideas of them under the form of space.

Time is likewise a law of intelligence rather than an entity in itself. As space is the form under which we relate a world of diversity to ourselves and each other, so time is the form under which we relate the world of experiences to the abiding self. Without this contribution of the self which survives the changes there could be no sense of time. In other words, it is because there is an element of timelessness in the thinker that he gets the idea of the passage of time. Time being the form under which intelligence acts, the mind by its own constitutive activity is able to grasp and assign a meaning to historic periods of which experience could tell it nothing.

The weakness in Kant's position lay in the fact that he took account only of the subjective side of this activity of the mind. It is well enough for me to say that time and space are only the forms under which I think, but are they peculiar to me? Do they not exist apart from my thinking? How may I be sure that the time and space which I think will correspond to that which others think? Kant's failure to answer these questions vitiated his system. It becomes at once apparent that both time and space must possess some objective validity to free them from the disjunctive caprice of the individual and make possible a world united in space and time relations. This Kant did not give us.

"We cannot impose mental forms upon the world of experience unless that world itself be adapted to those forms."[1]

It is interesting to note how Bowne, affirming the ideal nature of space and time, yet avoided the logical impasse to which Kant was brought. Bowne was too close to the practical in his thinking not to see that the forms of time and space must be true for the object of thought as well as for the thinker. To him space and time gain a validity which makes them universal for all intelligent beings through a Supreme Personal Intelligence who creates and upholds all. The world of things and of intelligences correspond each to each because all are comprehended in a Supreme Intelligence from which they acquire their meaning and reality.

WHERE CAN WE FIND A PERMANENT WORLD?

Of course Kant was not blind to the necessity of asserting somewhere an objective validity. He clearly saw that a purely subjective world would be one in which

---

[1] Bowne, Kant and Spencer, p. 150.

every man would make his own world and
no two worlds would correspond. It was
necessary to point out some principle that
would possess permanence and give unity.
This permanent principle he attempted to
introduce under what he called the analogies
of experience.[2] In this portion of the
Critique Kant becomes perilously involved
in his search for the permanent in phenomena. To find this principle of permanence he all but affirms an independent
and back-lying existence for things in
themselves. To the mind of Bowne the
problem of permanence could never be
solved in this crude fashion. "On the impersonal plane there is no possibility of
combining permanence with change, least
of all by a mere analysis of the notion of
change. On that plane we cannot reserve
anything in the world of change as an
abiding element, for as soon as it becomes
changeless it no longer explains change, and
when it explains change it passes into the
changing, and changes through and through.
The problem here can be solved only as we

carry it up to the plane of personality, and find the permanence of experience in the world of meaning and in the self-conscious intelligence which founds and administers the world of meanings under the forms of change."[3]

WHAT LIES BEHIND THE APPEARANCE OF THINGS?

The same subjectivity that oppressed Kant in the consideration of time and space troubled him likewise in his attempt to find the abiding real. This difficulty was in part due to his failure to discriminate between two possible definitions of the term "subjective." We may mean by the term that which is peculiar to the individual alone, or we may mean that which is true for intelligence anywhere and has no existence apart from it. If Kant had kept this truth in mind when affirming the subjectivity or phenomenal nature of reality, all might have been well. But failing to draw the distinction, he made the system of experience the fiction of the individual. Kant's

---

[3] Bowne, Kant and Spencer, pp. 99, 100.

only escape would have been to affirm a back-lying and independent Cause. It was only thus he could have saved his system from solipsism. Phenomena are not masks or appearances of any kind, existing only for the individual. They are the things that exist for human intelligences everywhere and derive their common meaning through a supreme intelligence by which they exist. We apprehend them through our own intelligence, but they do not depend upon our intelligence for their existence; and since they must depend upon intelligence for existence, it only remains that we affirm a back-lying intelligence as their cause and presupposition.[4]

But Kant does not discover the high road out of his subjectivism. For him things in succession imply causal relations, and as the causal relations in things must be something independent of the mind of the onlooker, there must be in phenomena a residuant reality beyond that which the mind is able to perceive. Thus he has resort to a doctrine of noumena. The end of this way is

---

[4] Bowne, Kant and Spencer, p. 124.

an impossible dualism, for it erects a reality which is not only independent of individual intelligence, but which is beyond all intelligence, being of a different and unknowable nature. This dualism into which Kant unwittingly falls is to be avoided by distinguishing between causal and phenomenal reality. Phenomenal reality is the noted succession of appearances, common to all. We can mark the preexistences and successions which universally hold in the world of experience, and we can formulate the law of their procedure without granting them a causal efficiency or saying anything about their metaphysical ground. Causal reality, in contrast, deals not with the order of succession, but with the ground of being itself.

Can We "Prove" the World of Spirit?

Kant's purpose was to prove that it is impossible from the common data of experience to arrive at affirmations respecting God and immortality. He did this, not from hostility, but from friendliness to faith.

Naturalism had shown the inadequacy of

the so-called "proofs" of the Divine existence. It went farther, for, assuming its
ability to account for everything in heaven
and in earth, it also asserted the non-
existence of everything not dreamt of in its
philosophy. What Kant did was to make
room for faith by showing that religious
convictions lie outside the province of the
naturalistic speculation. It could neither be
proved nor disproved on the basis of naturalism. Kant thus claims the honor of over-
throwing all materialistic and atheistic
teaching by showing its attempt at religious
explanation to be outside its possible field.
The religious world of to-day has come to
realize that there can be no "proofs" for
God and immortality, in the sense that was
so much sought after in Kant's day. We
realize now that the great argument for
God is the practical interest. We affirm
the existence of God because he is a necessity for all sane thinking and his existence
is demanded by the moral and religious
interests of life. This practical argument
possesses much more force for the present
day than the old "proofs." What is said

for the doctrine of God can likewise be said for immortality and all the fundamental religious truths. They stand forever because they are written into the very nature of the human spirit.

In his contention Kant was true to the facts. The apprehension of God is an act of faith. Spiritual truths are gained in the exercise of faith and the spiritual powers. Bowne, in a lecture commenting on Kant's showing of the impossibility of an intellectual demonstration of the existence of God, declared that the apprehension of God could be reached only by faith, and then added this significant word: "By way of mere speculation we cannot attain to demonstration in any field. There is no way of stopping where Kant stops."

The outcome of Kant's "antinomies of thought" after verbose and tedious discussion is closely allied to this pragmatic judgment upon the deeper religious values.

Bowne thus sums up his argument: "Conviction must be reached in life itself, and this has always, with scantiest exception, led the race to theistic faith, not, indeed, as something that can be speculatively demonstrated or against which any cavil or objection is impossible, but something which represents the line of least resistance for human thought. The intelligent world points to an intelligent author, the moral world to a moral author, the rational world to a rational author. This is the conclusion which the race has drawn and the conclusion in which it increasingly rests, the conclusion which it holds with more and more confidence as the ground of all its hope and the security of its efforts, whether in the field of science and cognition or of morality and religion. . . . Assuming the legitimacy of life and of our human instincts, we may ask ourselves what life implies; and Kant says it implies God, freedom, and immortality, as postulates without which the mind would fall into discord with itself and life would lose itself in inner contradiction. We may then hold these postulates, not as something given by the speculative reason, but as something rooted in life."[5]

---

[5] Bowne, Kant and Spencer, pp. 212, 213.

CHAPTER VII

THE ABSOLUTE PHILOSOPHY, LOTZE AND BOWNE

Is the World More than Knowledge?

Lotze was the first to successfully refute the absolute idealism of Hegel. Nevertheless, he was himself to be counted among the idealists. He hoped to harmonize the differences between modern scientific thought and that romantic idealism which had so largely characterized the metaphysics of the preceding generation. The interaction of things in an intelligible universe was to him the best evidence of essential unity between mind and matter. He believed that Hegel had indicated a great goal. He did not believe with Hegel that all truth can be deduced from reflection. It was Lotze's aim to grant perception, or empirical knowledge of nature, its place in thought.

"His philosophy is a persistent defense of perception against reflection, of the concrete particular against pale and vacant general ideas; it is a powerful protest against injustice to the individuality and uniqueness which he found at the core of every fact. Thought with its abstract conceptions and unsubstantial universals seemed to him poor and thin as compared with the facts and events of the real world; every general law seemed to him to fall short of reaching the core and essence of anything actual."[1]

In particular was Lotze opposed to the closed system of idealism where everything was so ordered in the eternal thought that there could by no possibility enter in any factors which had not already been determined before the world was, and which relegated freedom to the realm of shadow and make-believe. He believed that history was something more "than a translation in time of the eternally complete content of an ordered world." He concluded, then, that the world is something more than an eternal thought; that it contains a ca-

---

[1] Jones, Philosophy of Lotze, p. 9.

pacity for freedom and a possibility for the introduction of the unique, which is an irresistible demand of the human spirit. By his incisive criticisms he laid bare the deceptive generalities of the extreme Hegelian position and made necessary a drastic modification of its thought.

OF WHAT DOES REALITY CONSIST?

Hegelianism thought to reach reality by reflection and without the aid of experience. Lotze, on the other hand, held steadfastly to the importance of experience and maintained that we can understand it only as we grasp its inner continuity. He raised the question of the ultimate nature of reality by asserting that in a united universe of relations and correspondences capable of being apprehended it must be either material or spiritual. If we are to allow the reality of anything outside matter, the conclusion is foregone—the ultimate nature of being is spiritual. But if we are to understand reality, we need to know more than the elements into which it is divisible, more than the laws under which it acts; we must know also its destination. Laws in themselves are nothing more than the formulated sequence of events, the tabulated data of experience. They can give us little concerning the ground of their activity. We must go back of the law to the apparent aim of the uniformity and therein catch a glimpse of the controlling purpose. Thus he introduces into his system the idea of value. He now proceeds to describe reality as the realized law of procedure. It is that in which the Infinite Purpose is realizing itself.

So far Lotze has scarcely escaped the absolute idealism which he aimed to supersede. His world of reality remains phenomenal in spite of his protestations. This phenomenalism he endeavored to avoid by looking toward the Good as the supreme end. "The objectivity of knowledge consists in this, that it is not a meaningless play of illusion, but that it presents to us a world whose several parts are linked and ordered according to the prescription of that which is alone real in the world, namely, the good."[2]

---

[2] Quoted by Stählin, Kant, Lotze and Ritschl, p. 141.

Thus with Lotze the Supreme Good is the ultimate Reality in whose existence all other realities find their ground.

Bowne's Debt to Lotze

There are many well-defined correspondences between the systems of Lotze and Bowne. There are many points at which Bowne would gladly have owned his obligation to his teacher. An examination of these correspondences will be of moment to those who are interested in Bowne's philosophy.

They were at one in the insistence upon the difference between the practical field of science and the speculative field of metaphysics, in which both hark back to Kant. They held that science is properly limited to the order of coexistence and sequence in phenomena with reference to the practical issues. To metaphysics alone is assigned the realm of efficient causality. The scientist may learn from experience with phenomena the laws of their action and interaction, but when he goes back of phenomena to discuss the nature of reality or being, he has left the realm of science for that of philosophy.

Both discerned the folly of an attempt to understand nature simply by a method of classification. They called attention to the emptiness of such endeavors so far as the problem of reality is concerned. Classification is a method of intelligence the better to handle its materials. Classification in no wise changes the things classified or reveals their back-lying reality.

Both philosophers pointed out the astounding claims of atomism to an efficiency which in the end would endow each separate atom with a purpose, wisdom, and knowledge of other atoms far superior to human intelligence, and with a proclivity for peace remarkable in this, that in a divided world of innumerable atoms there should be any working in relations at all. Instead of naturalism being free from the dark realm of magic and unaccountable powers, she is rather the high priestess of superstition with her powerful demiurges of atoms.

They saw the impossibility of assuming the absentee God of absolute idealism.

Such a God would find himself, at the best, working at cross purposes in a disjointed world, and gradually realizing his thought through the slow-struggling intelligence of man and accomplishing his own moral character in the slower moving ebb and flow of the tides of human action.

They saw that neither pluralism which springs from atomism nor the pantheism which springs from Absolutism was sufficient to explain the world and leave place on the one hand for individuality and on the other for freedom.

They were alike in recognizing the absurdities which left Absolutism in the clouds. Lotze felt himself to be sufficiently definite when he referred everything to the Supreme Good. Bowne went on to declare that the world of experience can be maintained as real only as it is grounded in a Supreme Personality from whom all things forever proceed.

Bowne possessed Lotze's view concerning the barren round of mechanical causation assumed by materialism, in which there can be no possibility of progress, no chance for the introduction of unique factors of advance. They were one likewise in recognition of the corresponding weakness of an Absolute who contained all in himself, and in whom was buried also all possibility of human freedom, that novelty that forever spells progress in the history of the individual and the race.

BOWNE'S ADVANCE ON LOTZE'S SYSTEM

It is only fair to say that Bowne received many of the features of his system from Lotze. In the clearness of his critical faculties he was remarkably like Lotze. It is also fair to say that Bowne overcame the weaknesses inherent in Lotze's system and carried it out to a more logical conclusion.

In his definition of reality, Lotze is needlessly vague. His shortest and most direct definition of reality is that it is the realized law of procedure. This definition points toward activism, but it is not thoroughgoing enough. Its reality is still phenomenal, existing only in the absolute purpose. What he was aiming for was a reality whose realness lay in the very act of a Divine Purpose realizing itself.

Bowne's definition of reality was not only more clear and simple, but also more profound. With him reality is that which can act or be acted upon. Thus he makes way for matter and mind and God.

Lotze pointed out the fact that we must discover some continuity behind the ebb and flow of matter and even of human experience if we are to find out the meaning of the world. Bowne carried the thought up to secure footing and made the relation of thought and thing clear. He affirmed that the desired continuity can be found alone in personality. Personality is the only power of which we are conscious that can join the sundered experiences of time and space into a unity and look upon all from the standpoint of the one. Thus alone, he argues, is unity possible in the world. The universe finds its unity in the thought of a Supreme Personality, himself the unchanging cause of change.

Thus Lotze's vague Purpose of the Supreme Good, which he considers the fundamental reality, gives way to a Person who is also the World-Ground. Both the material universe and the individual mind fall into step because both proceed from the same source. Our intelligences were made for the true understanding of the world. What the general mind reports is true because the world was made for our intelligence. In this way the idea with which Lotze began was given a new and richer and more powerful content.

If Lotze had thus completed his system, he would have been free from the criticism of one of the most skillful and friendly critics, who declared that his cardinal defect lay at this point. This writer says: "He may, like the ordinary consciousness, maintain the necessity of nature, and the freedom of men, and the omnipresence of God; he may give man all his own way, which is essential to morality, and God all His own way, which is essential to religion, and thus permit both these forces which mold the higher destinies of mankind to exist together. But he must also strive to reconcile them. Truth for him must not be a thing of aspects and phases merely; he must not agree with the common consciousness in its fragmentariness."[3]

Herein is the chief point of difference between Lotze and Bowne. Lotze stops short of asserting personality of the World-Ground and leaves the fundamental reality only less vague than Hegel's absolute. Bowne presses on to the assertion of personality in the World-Ground with all that such an assertion implies. He thus carries the metaphysical problem up into religion and is able thereby to bring about that very reconciliation between science and religion which was Lotze's own aim.

Bowne's position is well disclosed in a passage in his last work touching the idealist position, in which he says: "Being in this world is nothing more than having a certain form and type of experience with certain familiar conditions. Passing out of this world into another would mean simply not a transition through space, but passing into a new form and type of experience differently constituted from the present. And

[3] Jones, Philosophy of Lotze, p. 13.

how many of these systems are possible or to what extent this change might go is altogether beyond us. Of course these many systems would all be objectively founded; that is, they would be rooted in the will and purpose of the Creator, and they would also be one in the sense that the creative purpose would comprise them all in one plan; but they would not be one in the sense of being phases or aspects of one absolute reality. They would be stages in God's unfolding plan, but not aspects of the static universe. This static universe is a phantom of abstract thought. The only reality is God and his progressively unfolding plan and purpose and work, and the world of finite spirits. In this case also we should have a relativity but not an illusion, a validity of knowledge within the sphere which finds its ground and warrant in the plan and purpose of the Creator."[4]

---

[4] Bowne, Kant and Spencer, pp. 145, 146.

SECTION III
PRAGMATISM

CHAPTER VIII

THE UNMETAPHYSICAL PRAGMA-TISM OF WILLIAM JAMES

THE PRAGMATIC ELEMENT IN THE HISTORY OF PHILOSOPHY

PROTAGORAS is said to have been the originator of the watchword of pragmatism —"Man is the measure of all things." The phrase and the doctrine have unpleasant connections, however, for Protagoras and the Sophists to whose school he belonged meant thereby all that the word "sophism" has come to imply in modern life. In the words of Eucken, "Man the measure of all things," meant for them "A renunciation of all universally valid standards, a surrender of truth to man's momentary caprice and fluctuating inclinations. In other words, it implied that everything may be turned this way or that and differently judged, according to the point of view; that what appears as the right may be represented as the wrong, and conversely; and that any cause may be championed according to the necessities of the case or to one's whim. In this manner life is gradually degraded into a means of the profit, the self-indulgence, even the sport of the single individual, who acknowledges no restraints, feels no respect; . . . thus the good yields to the profitable; all valuations become relative. . . . Such a doctrine of relativity . . . raised to a sovereign position, . . . becomes the deadly enemy of everything great and true."[1]

The pragmatic movement came in Greece after the climax of her brilliant age had passed. The touch of disorganization and decay had struck into her civilization. Old faiths and old institutions were breaking before an incoming tide of individualism.

That system which had such questionable origin with the Sophists became with the Stoics a judgment by moral values, and here perhaps reached its highest and noblest influence. It appears in the sensualistic

---

[1] Eucken, The Problem of Human Life, p. 14.

system of Epicurus, to whom the criterion
of truth becomes the sensation of pleasure
as contrasted with pain.[2]

We again see the pragmatic postulate in
the teachings of Pyrrho and the new acad-
emy. They hold it as the foundation of
knowledge. Arcesilaus named probabilism as
the only rule of practical life. Carneades
introduced the idea of degrees of proba-
bility. To the eclectics, that was truth
which appeared to be true. In the end,
when both scientific and deductive truth
have been rid of all reality, we reach the
reaction of neo-platonism with its affirmation of truth by revelation alone.

Modern pragmatism applies the thought
of value, not primarily to the moral and
æsthetic, as did the Stoics, but to reality
itself. Davidson has called attention to the
fact that the new element in modern pragmatism is to bring knowledge as well as
æsthetics and ethics to the test of practical
value.[3] The modern pragmatists do not by

---

[2] Compare Janet and Seailles, History of the Problems of
Philosophy, p. 103.

[3] The Stoic Creed, p. 256.

any means agree in the phase of the system which is most important. Mr. Pierce revived the name for modern philosophy. F. C. S. Schiller is interested in giving the movement a particularly subjectivistic turn. James has pursued the line of Realism. Because of the extended influence of the latter, and the commonness with which his name is associated with the term "pragmatism," we shall confine ourselves to the discussion of his particular system.

CAN THE PRAGMATIC TEST OF TRUTH BE MAINTAINED?

In the chapter on "The Notion of Truth," in his volume on pragmatism, James justly balks at the vague abstractions of the definition of truth given by the rationalists. He quotes Taylor's definition, "Truth is the system of propositions which have an unconditional claim to be recognized as valid," and also Rickert's statement that "Truth is a name for all those judgments which we find ourselves under obligations to make by a kind of imperative duty." These definitions of truth James declares "unutterable triviality." While we sympathize with him in his revolt from any attempt at making truth a mere abstraction, we cannot be blind to the commission of the same error of abstraction by James himself when he substitutes "verify-able" for "verify-cation" under exigency. What both James and his rationalist opponents are aiming for is an independent norm of truth. This fact James desired to conceal while the rationalists openly admitted it. By "verify-able" James means that there is a common-to-all which makes it possible for the individual to compare his judgment with the common judgment of others. Thus only can he push the borders of knowledge past his individual experiences to truths imparted by others and which he might verify if circumstances permitted. He could better have shown the error of the rationalist definition of truth by calling attention to its fallacy of the abstract. He would also have secured the desired concreteness by open acknowledgment of a common-to-all in human experience by which the individual can verify his own conclusions respecting phenomena.

But Mr. James tells us that there is no such thing as truth independent, and by this, if he is consistent, he means truth independent of concrete individual experience. He declares, "The pragmatist clings to facts and concreteness, observes truth at its work in particular cases, and generalizes." He does not, however, show us the "value" of this generalization in a world in which truth is to be found only in concrete individual cases. How is the pragmatist to possess any certainty that his intellectual effort of synthesis represents any corresponding reality? Indeed, it could not apart from a higher and uniting intelligence.

Again he says, "True ideas are those that we can assimilate, validate, corroborate, and verify. False ideas are those we cannot." Here, moving on the individualistic plane, are certain difficulties that give no promise of solution. The jungle-dweller who is told for the first time that the earth is round might be utterly unable either to assimilate, validate, corroborate, or verify the statement. Would his inability in this respect justify him in putting the conception of rotundity in the region of false ideas? Would the truth thereby be imperiled? Still there are some who profess to believe that the roundness of the earth would remain presumably beyond question. It would seem to come perilously close to being a truth independent of this man's concrete individual experience. It might conceivably be beyond the concrete individual experience of any dweller upon the earth, as in the days before the rotundity of the earth was discovered. Was or was it not true? Would the earth continue round in the absence of human life and intelligence?

Evidently, the chief pragmatist himself was troubled with evil dreams, for a few pages later he declares that "verify-ability" will do as well as "verify-cation" anyway. Here he jumps again from the particular to the general without sensing it. If he would rescue truth from the uncertainties of individual experiences, he could do so by positing a Personality as the World-Ground. He could thus have saved his pragmatism and have maintained his ground against rationalism.

Respecting his definition of truth as that which serves an end or a purpose, Davidson[4] very justly calls attention to the fact that purpose or end implies an intellectual element at utter variance with the pragmatic claim that it is not man's intellect or reason which determines reality and truth, but his will and his feelings.

So the pragmatic definition of truth, while attempting to avoid the abstractions of absolute idealism, becomes the prey of a solipsistic individualism, because, spurning the assistance of metaphysics, it has no intelligent ground. At any rate, the serious-minded cannot be satisfied with a test of value for truth which shall be merely human and relative. "We have outgrown the standard of a welfare merely human, and all the values of such a welfare cannot blind us to their narrowness and emptiness."[5]

ARE SPACE AND TIME THE ABIDING REALITIES?

Unwilling to affirm any continuity which falls outside the realm of concrete indi-

[4] The Stoic Creed, p. 263.
[5] Eucken, Knowledge and Life, p. 83.

vidual experience, because that would be untrue to pragmatism, James is forced to seek some continuity which will hold his disunited and pluralistic world together long enough to consider the situation. This continuity he gains in a thoroughly naturalistic way by assuming time and space as the abiding realities. "Space and time are thus vehicles of continuity by which the world's parts hang together."[6] One must think of space and time both as objectively real. Of them he says: "Just as atoms, not half or quarter atoms, are the minimum of matter that can be, and every finite amount of matter contains a finite number of atoms, so any amounts of time, space, change, etc., which we might assume would be composed of a finite number of minimal amounts of time, space, and change."[7]

One scarcely knows whether to be more surprised at the naïve boldness in presenting such crudities or the uncritical state of the mind that could formulate them. In the first place, the unseeable and imaginary

---

[6] James, Pragmatism, p. 134.

[7] Some Problems of Philosophy, p. 154.

atom is reduced in words to finite and ponderable reality. Then such subjective ideas as space and time are spoken of as if they could be reckoned in the same way. If there is any meaning, it would seem as if one might trade a chunk of his space for another's time, and so prolong life by reducing the dimensions of his "verify-able" world.

The resulting mystification regarding the nature of time is shown in his view of the verification of history by the individual. He says: "The stream of time can be remounted only verbally, or verified indirectly by the present prolongations or effects of what the past harbored. Yet if they agree with these verbalities and effects, we can know that our ideas of the past are true. *As true as past time itself was,* so true was Julius Cæsar, so true were antediluvian monsters, all in their proper dates and settings."[8]

Truth being confined to concrete individual experience by Mr. James's fundamental postulate, it would seem easier to

---

[8] Pragmatism, pp. 214, 215.

take his say-so for the foregoing than to attempt to reach any consistent ground for such a view of time.

The fact is that time is nothing apart from an abiding personality to relate its flowing events each to each and all to some unmoving center. But once this is granted, the disunited world in time and space falls into wondrous unity which would be quite upsetting to the pluralistic mind, which the pluralistic mind will not acknowledge but without which it cannot think. He should have become aware that the "connecting medium" was no less than personality when he talks about the relationships of life breaking up into little worlds, or a multitude of small systems.

Pluralism a Confession of Failure to Unite Subject and Object

Being unable from the empirical standpoint to found any real unity, James turns to pluralism as a means of escape from the insistent problems arising out of the contrast between mind and matter, subject and object. The mere thought of any essential unity seems repugnant. He says, "If our intellect had been as much interested in disjunctive as it is in conjunctive relations, philosophy would have equally successfully celebrated the world's disunion."[9] "Ay, there's the rub . . . what dreams!" Why is the intellect not equally interested in establishing a disjunctive world? The reason is a very good one. It is because it is as mentally impossible to seriously think a disjunctive world as to think a topsy-turvy world. If we can find no higher unity, it will inevitably be this, that there is a world of various relations all of which are grasped by our intelligence and are thought of as "our" world. Even pragmatists are driven to this common expedient before they can tell us what pragmatism and pluralism are. The fact that the world can be understood by us is a principle of unity in itself, which must be removed before pluralism can be admitted. Unity does not depend, as the pragmatists seem to think, upon chemical spatial and social interaction between given individuals. The apple does not quarrel

---

[9] Pragmatism, p. 137.

with the banana because both cannot grow on the same tree nor in the same climate. They are not for that reason parts of other and disunited worlds. They both find a unity in the comprehension of very ordinary mortals as being in the same world and in spite of diversity yielding obedience to the same laws.

CAN PRAGMATIC PLURALISM REACH FREEDOM OR SOLVE THE PROBLEM OF EVIL?

One reason that Mr. James assigned for denying a unitary world was to save some place in it for novelty and innovation.[10] The effort to escape the meshes of absolutism on the one hand, and to avoid the necessities of empiricism on the other, so as to gain a place in the world for freedom, is a laudable one. But here pluralism offers only a false hope. The common example of absolute innovation in our world is that which is introduced by the free human spirit. The moment a free intelligence is posited as the world ground we have our freedom and not in any otherwise.

---

[10] Some Problems in Philosophy, p. 132.

In similar manner pluralism congratulates itself on having escaped the problem of evil. It escapes it in the sense that having neither God nor absolute the presence of the problem need not be accounted for as a moral obligation. But in the very same terms whereby it escapes the problem it also makes void all moral responsibility in the individual. If that is truth which the individual sees at the moment—and we must hold pluralistic pragmatism to its principles here—then any independent norm of right moral action is as ridiculous as the abstractions of idealism. The maintenance of laws and the punishment of offenders against such ideal right is involved in the same category. What the individual sees for the moment is the true and the good. The individual cannot be blamed for not seeing other than as it presents itself to him. Along with the heralded escape from the problem of evil has come likewise the escape from moral responsibility. One is reminded of what Professor Eucken says of the moral degradation which followed in the wake of the sophistic pragmatism and which was quoted in the early part of this chapter. Of course Mr. James did not intend this result, for in another place he criticizes materialism because it rules out the moral order of the world.[11]

Yet with all his love for a disunited world, Mr. James seems to tell us of a certain sort of unity, a unity of nature that is coming to pass gradually in proportion as we verify our ideas. It would be difficult to explain such a unity except as a subjective and intellectual one, as the mind reaches conclusions, classifies and generalizes its knowledge. But we have already been warned to abhor all intellectualism, so that even this poor attempt at unity would seem to be denied to a consistent pragmatist.

The whole subject of pluralism has thus been summed up by a recent writer, who says: "As regards pragmatism, it does not furnish us with a pluralistic universe, but

---

[11] Pragmatism, pp. 105–107. For a discussion of the relation of the Scholastic Free Thinkers to Pragmatism in judging religion by its utility, politically, morally, and socially, and the affirmation that this is the necessary outcome of any pragmatism not theistically grounded, see Lange, History of Materialism, vol. i, pp. 222ff.

with a thinker who interrupts his thinking, an experimenter who breaks off his experiment, whenever it suits his feelings. Pragmatistic thought resembles the artist's thought, in so far as both not only build for the Heart's Desire, but also (as Omar Khayyám forgot to mention) break off and sweep away its own construction whenever the logical necessities, that is, the *peculiarities independent of his wishes*, begin to bore or annoy it. The pluralistic pragmatist takes advantage of the fact (for even he must build with facts!) that we need not always *think on and on*, that there are other subjects and other points of view; in short, that although the independent universe rolls on in its established manner, with or without the music of the spheres and the hymn of Goethe's archangels, human attention can turn upon its ear and for a while dream of its own juicy cabbages or intoxicating effulgent roses."[12]

In commenting on Plato's search for the absolute, Eucken has given in clear statement the argument against all such prag-

---

[12] Vernon Lee, Vital Lies, vol. ii, pp. 171, 172.

matic schemes of life. "Every human undertaking which seeks to be self-sufficient, and to avoid all responsibility to superior authority, he looks upon as petty and necessarily inadequate. Dominated by a hollow show of independence, such efforts can never produce more than the appearance of virtue and happiness, which is rendered repulsive by its self-complacency. . . . However much that is problematic may remain in Plato's Doctrine of Ideas, the latter discloses a great truth which we cannot relinquish. And that is the recognition of the fact that there is *a realm of truth beyond the likes and dislikes of men;* that truths are valid, not because of our consent, but independently of it, and in a sphere raised above all human opinion and power. Such a conviction is the foundation of the independence of science, and of the secure upbuilding of civilization; only a self-dependent truth can provide laws and norms which elevate human existence because they unite it."[13]

---

[13] Eucken, Problem of Human Life, pp. 18-21.

CHAPTER IX

BOWNE'S PRAGMATISM, "A STEP IN THE DEVELOPMENT OF PHIL-OSOPHY"

A Pragmatic Definition of Being

F. C. S. Schiller, in attacking the absolutist idea of God from the pragmatic standpoint, declares that the pragmatic dependence of meaning on purpose "negatives the notion that truth can depend on how things would appear to an all-embracing, or 'absolute' mind. For such a mind could have no purpose. It could not, that is, select part of its content as an object of special interest to be operated upon or aimed at. In human minds, on the other hand, meaning is always selective and purposive."[1]

Bowne is equally antagonistic to the closed system of the absolutist. He too re-

---

[1] Schiller, Humanism, p. 10.

fused to accept a pantheistic God appearing in all his creations and depending upon them for his own being, hence thinking evil with their evil thoughts and bound to a hideous and unethical world which really is himself. But we must take note of what Schiller's interpretation does to the system. With him truth becomes thoroughly individualistic. One man's "truth" is on as secure a footing as another's. One man's illusions, he being the judge of his truth, are as valid as the most plausible conclusions of another. Schiller seems to feel that there cannot be an independent norm of truth, apart from Absolutism. In the endeavor to get away from all ideas of truth as an abstraction he makes void the value of concrete and particular truth.

Bowne retains his pragmatism, and shows the emptiness of the absolute position without surrendering truth that shall be valid for all. He does this through his definition of being. We have already noted his definition of the real as that which can act or be acted upon. The definition of being naturally follows. It is neither an Abstract

Supreme Idea, nor an Unknowable substance as the base of phenomena. Being is implied in the capacity for intelligent causal action, or the capacity of being intelligently acted upon. He would join with the pragmatists in saying that there is no being apart from purpose, meaning, by that, intelligent purpose. All that exists, then, is the result or manifestation of a supreme active or purposive intelligence and includes the world of lesser intelligences. It has no meaning apart from this intelligence, which is its ground. Mind can understand the movement of matter because both proceed from the same ground. The mind grasps the meaning of the world because it owns a kinship with the intelligence that creates the world. It is itself purposive and self-directing within the world-order. This definition of being escapes the pantheistic conclusion of absolutism and also avoids the mechanical determinism of empiricism.

All being is, then, according to Bowne, essentially causal and active.[2] In reaching this conclusion he guards his position by a

[2] For discussion see Bowne, Metaphysics, p. 17.

very important discrimination between phenomenal or inductive as contrasted with metaphysical efficiency, which is the immanent causality of a Fundamental Unitary Being. Phenomenal causality refers to the laws of change in phenomena which give us the anticipated order of events of science. These may be studied, classified, and verified without reference to their metaphysical ground. Metaphysical efficiency has reference to that Supreme Intelligent Purpose by which all things subsist, and which must be affirmed if there is to be any true knowledge or if the sundered sides of consciousness are to be united.[3]

The Escape from Pluralism and Absolutism to World-Unity

Convinced that there can be no unity without a closed system, with no real freedom and no novelty, the pluralists have rushed to the maintenance of a disjunctive universe. But a disjunctive universe is as much of an impossibility to thought in a sane and intelligible world as a universe

---

[3] Ibid., pp. 83–90.

absolutely predetermined by a Supreme Idea or by the mechanical necessities of materialism. The refuge taken in a pluralistic universe is simply the attempt to flee from one irrationality to a greater. We find pluralism unable to reconcile change and identity on its impersonal plane. The demon of determinism may be momentarily exorcised, but with the resulting return of seven other demons worse than itself. In maintaining a pluralistic universe the pluralist does not make it disjunctive enough to be consistent. Unless he preserves a certain amount of unity, the unity of a mind able to grasp the fleeting events of time and the baffling appearances of change, all knowledge would be meaningless. Even pluralism would become a jargon of words. The baseless fears of pluralism spring from a failure adequately to define the meaning of unity. Bowne[4] points out the fact that the only real unity of which we are directly aware is the unity of the free and conscious self. The self survives the passing events of experience, relates them to itself under

[4] Metaphysics, p. 91.

the forms of time and space, and makes itself the center of a multitudinous and rapidly changing world. That there is any higher unity than this synthesis of the world by the individual is due to the fact that one is not alone in the universe of intelligence, but is surrounded by a world of self-conscious intelligences which are themselves comprehended in synthesis by a Supreme Personal Intelligence. Through self-conscious and self-acting personality alone can the world be brought into substantial unity. The experiences of the individual, then, become something more than peculiar to himself and valid for more than himself. Living in a world of intelligences, which is maintained by intelligence, his idea of truth must conform, not only to the common-to-all, but, higher than this, to the order of an intelligible world. Thus at a single stroke are we rid of the conflict between mind and matter, noumena and phenomena, and the disjointed and illogical world of pluralism. This is done also without resort to an idealism which, though grand in its conception, is death to the maintenance of freedom and individuality. How strongly Bowne felt toward the outcome of such a system may be judged by his own words:

"When we consider life at all reflectively, we come upon two facts. First, we have thoughts and feelings and volitions; and these are our own. We also have a measure of self-control, or the power of self-direction. Here, then, in experience we find a certain selfhood and a relative independence. This fact constitutes us real persons, or, rather, it is the meaning of our personality. The second fact is that we cannot regard this life as self-sufficient and independent. How the life is possible we do not know; we only know that it is. How the two facts are put together is altogether beyond us. We only know that we cannot interpret life without admitting both, and that to deny either lands us in contradiction and nonsense. It is no doubt fine, and in some sense it is correct, to say that God is in all things; but when it comes to saying that God is all things, and that all forms of thought and feeling and conduct are his, then reason simply commits suicide. God thinks and feels in what we call our thinking and feeling; and hence he blunders in our blundering and is stupid in our stupidity. He contradicts himself also with the utmost freedom; for a deal of his thinking does not hang together from one person to another, or from one day to another in the same person. Error, folly, and sin are all made divine; and reason and conscience as having authority vanish. The only thing that is not divine in this scheme is God; and he vanishes into a congeries of contradictions and basenesses."[5]

THE IDEAL NATURE OF TIME AND SPACE

Next to his doctrine of a Supreme Intelligence as the World-Ground, Bowne is most likely to be denied standing as a Pragmatist because of his position regarding the ideal nature of time and space. Pragmatism of the James type is very prone to fly at anything which bears the suggestion of idealism. Such pragmatism approaches the problems from a realistic if not from a

[5] Bowne, Metaphysics, p. 102.

materialistic standpoint. Nevertheless, the question of the nature of time and space is a momentous one for the cause of pluralistic pragmatism. We have already seen, with Mr. James, how purely objective is their explanation. Space is a sort of entity existing for itself, and time is of similar nature, to be spoken of as if it possessed extension. Mr. James seems to indicate that we are sure of the events of history because time as an enduring entity pokes itself somewhat like a pole into the present. Seeing one end, the present, we can be sure there is another end, though out of sight. It is not surprising that the pragmatists are unwilling to surrender space and time to idealism, for on these two hang all the unity that is left them, and by their own confession some unity is necessary even to a pluralistic universe.

But to consider the question of history, what is there in my present that reminds me of the historic character, Julius Cæsar, or compels me to believe that any such person ever lived? What realistic way is there of being sure that he existed in his

time as I in mine? To arrive at such a
conclusion I must rationalize and relate, and
this is strictly forbidden by the pragmatic
doctrine. Indeed, I can have no idea of
the time that has elapsed since Cæsar's day,
being myself confined to my threescore
years and ten. But I relate events to my
own personality in time, and by imagination I relate other events and other days of
which I am told, in some sort of consistent
order to that time into which my own life
falls. By the same token I am able to relate
my present time to a fancied order yet to
come, and obtain a belief in it only second
to that which obtains concerning that which
is told me as history.

Without a unitary personality the fleeting
facts and changes of our human life could
not be related. To-day would have no intelligible relation to yesterday, only that an
abiding personality superior to the events,
possessing a certain timelessness, relates
them to itself. Likewise can we think of
the events of history only as they might be
the related experiences of a unitary being
itself above their flux and change.

The Pragmatic Test for Religious Values

James, speaking of the pragmatic test as applied to religion, says: "If theological ideas prove to have a concrete value for life, they will be true, for pragmatism, in the sense of being good for so much. For how much more they are true will depend entirely on their relations to the other truths that also have to be acknowledged. . . . The true is the name of whatever proves itself to be good in the way of belief, and good too for definite assignable reasons."[6] Permission to exist in the pragmatic scheme is of little value to religion, however, in a many sundered world. Without a fundamental intelligence, capable also of moral qualities, with a care for moral law binding on all moral creatures, one's theological beliefs—indeed, one's ideal of the good—becomes momentary and individual. The belief which is found to be true for one man will be found equally false for another. There could be under such a system no common moral imperative to receive the

[6] Pragmatism, pp. 73, 76.

sanction of all moral beings. Yet this is one of the common experiences in life.

Bowne applied the pragmatic test to religion, but from a very different standpoint. Affirming a moral governor of the world, he yet held that the test of theological opinion, of so-called religious experience, must ever lie in actual life. "How does it work in life?" was a question proper to any religious belief whatever. By the practical answer must the theory stand or fall.

On the other hand, those beliefs that have been found contributing toward a higher civilization, a nobler moral order, a clearer conception of duty and the greatest good to the race, carry with them their own credentials, which cannot be speculatively overthrown.

SECTION IV
BOWNE AND SOME PRESENT-DAY THINKERS

CHAPTER X

BERGSON, THE ABSTRACTIONS OF AN IMPERSONAL PHILOSOPHY

CAN KNOWLEDGE AND LIFE BE BROUGHT TOGETHER ON THE EMPIRICAL BASIS?

BERGSON approaches the problems of philosophy from the standpoint of empiricism. He denies the conclusions of idealism and at the same time opposes the claims of materialism. He says: "We maintain as against materialism, that perception overflows infinitely the cerebral state; but we have endeavored to establish as against idealism, that matter goes in every direction beyond our representation of it, a representation which the mind has gathered out of it, so to speak, by an intelligent choice. Of these two opposite doctrines, the one attributes to the body and the other to the intellect a true power of creation, the first insisting that our brain begets representation and the second that our understanding designs the plan of nature. And against these two doctrines we invoke the same testimony, that of consciousness, which shows us our body as one image among others and our understanding as a certain faculty of dissociating, of distinguishing, of opposing logically, but not of creating or of constructing."[1]

He states the problem of philosophy to be the bringing together of the sundered sides of consciousness, matter and mind, life and knowledge, and discloses the fatal flaw in the Spencerian system: "It is necessary that these two inquiries, theory of knowledge and theory of life, should join each other. . . . Together they may solve by a method more sure, brought nearer to experience, the great problems that philosophy poses. For if they should succeed in their common enterprise, they would show us the formation of the intellect, and thereby the genesis of that matter of which our intellect traces the general configuration. They would dig to the very

---

[1] Matter and Memory, p. 236.

PROBLEMS OF PHILOSOPHY

root of nature and of mind. They would substitute for the false evolutionism of Spencer—which consists of cutting up present reality already evolved, into little bits no less evolved, and then recomposing it with these fragments, thus positing in advance everything that is to be explained—a true evolutionism, in which reality would be followed in its generation and its growth."[2]

Of being, Bergson says, "Being, in ourselves, is becoming, progress and growth."[3] Being is, then, a part of the act of consciousness, matter and mind conjoined in perception. The consciousness, freighted with all its past, comes to the act of perception in the present. This activity, the consonance of being and knowing, is the very essence of reality.

What Bergson is seeking after is something more than mechanical causation that would make thought the mere product of material forces, while, on the other hand, he seeks to establish a world which shall

[2] Creative Evolution, p. xiii, f.
[3] Sc. Le Roy, Philosophy of Bergson, p. 38.

147

not be dependent on the individual judgment. A world of mechanical causation is a closed system and negates the reality of knowledge. A world which must search for its reality in a Divine Idea alone takes away all possibility of novelty or uniqueness. Bergson sees that there is a factor of which neither side has taken account, the factor of novelty, without which there can be no progress or evolution. This factor he introduces under the name of "vital impulse," which he makes the seat of reality.

Does he, then, reach the goal for which he has striven—the unity of mind and matter, of knowledge and life? He has if we are to accept his word as the final authority in the matter. But his position contains certain important implications that vitiate the system.

Time as Duration

To escape the Spencerian snare of mechanical explanation, Bergson gives to the idea of time as duration the leading role in his philosophy. Instead of time being, on the one hand, an external reality upon which are strung successive experiences, or, on the other, a relating of experiences by an abiding personality as with Bowne, Bergson takes a position less clear, that the individual contains within himself the past at any moment. Duration is not a mere succession of appearances, but himself, his individuality. His stock illustration of this is the rolling snowball: "My mental state," he says, "as it advances on the road of time, is continually swelling with the duration which it accumulates; it goes on increasing—rolling upon itself, as a snowball on the snow."[4] "The past follows us at every instant; all that we have thought, felt, and willed from our earliest infancy is there, leaning over the present which is about to join it, pressing against the portals of consciousness that would fain leave it outside. . . . What are we, in fact, what is our character, if not the condensation of the history we have lived from our birth—nay, even before our birth, since we bring with us prenatal dispositions."[5]

---

[4] Creative Evolution, p. 2.
[5] Creative Evolution, pp. 4, 5.

To understand the implication of this doctrine it is necessary to pause and ask ourselves a few pertinent questions. Granted that time is but a bastard space, and is nothing apart from experience. Is it not something apart from my individual experience? Granted that I derive my sense of duration from my own past states. What gives me power to go beyond my individual experience? If time is nothing apart from individual experiences, how can any two of us come by the same calendar? Why does my time coincide with yours? Why is my sense of time greater, the fewer the experiences that fill my day, and shorter, the more multiplied these experiences? If this duration is myself and at the same time a consciousness, why is it that all memories are not with me at the same moment, and all are not equally at my command? How does attention come in to fix some events indelibly in my mind while I may deliberately choose to reject others? Is not this power of choice, this principle of freedom, something apart from the mere consciousness, possessing in itself the power of direction? How, having never experienced it in consciousness, can I exercise the historical sense?

To avoid the deadlock raised by such questions as these, we are told of racial memories passed along from generation to generation. Much language is used to describe an imaginary stream or current of life. We have been warned to beware of abstraction in speaking of life, but now it seems expedient to say: "At a certain moment, at certain points in space, a visible current has taken rise; this current of life, traversing the bodies it has organized one after another, passing from generation to generation, has become divided amongst species and distributed amongst individuals without losing anything of its force."[6] Thus have we fallen into that very fallacy of abstraction against which Bergson had warned us.

If there is a racial memory which flows along with and is a part of this current of life, just what is it, speaking concretely? It remains to be proved that we can inherit

---

[6] Creative Evolution, p. 26.

the intellectual ideas of our ancestors. More's the pity for many of us. But it seems reasonable to say that there can be no experience apart from an experiencing intelligence. How, then, can the experiences of my own immediate ancestors, not to mention those of my cousins and my aunts, become the property of my consciousness until they are grasped through an effort of my intelligence? Here it is evident our progress was only verbal.

Further: if time is duration, we must ask, "For whom?" Events can be gathered up and related only by a consciousness which not only endures, but is also a self-relating personality. This personality can relate itself to events outside of its experience only as they and it find relation through a higher, self-relating Personality, which is not fragmentary, but which knows all.

THE "VITAL IMPULSE" ASSUMED FOR THE SAKE OF FREEDOM

To free the individual from becoming a mere mechanism whose present is the product of past states, and to give place to initiative, Bergson introduces the factor which he calls the "vital impulse." He says: "The role of life is to insert some indetermination into matter. Indeterminate, i. e., unforeseeable, are the forms it creates in the course of its evolution."[7] It is the "vital impulse" which gives rise to new possibilities. It is the source and explanation of evolution. Instead of a closed mechanical universe, we have one in which any miracle may occur. While avoiding a universe of mechanism on the one hand, and a fore-ordered world on the other, he seems to choose a world in which God himself cannot know what is going to happen.

It is difficult to see how in such a scheme it is possible to preserve any order of nature whatever. All purpose, order, or predictableness is especially horrifying as implying a closed system and an absence of freedom. The "vital impulse" raised to the power of a self-directive intelligent personality would give ground, not only for freedom, but also for the usual order of

[7] Creative Evolution, p. 126.

phenomena. The very order of occurrence would be based upon such a Supreme Will. By gaining freedom without such a Personality Bergson undoes the possibility of a unitary world of relations. This conclusion has been very well brought out by the criticism of a well-known writer: "If for the magic power of types invoked by Aristotle we substituted, with M. Bergson, the magic power of the *'elan vital,'* that is, of evolution in general, we should be referring events not to finer, more familiar, more pervasive processes, but to one all-embracing process, unique and always incomplete. Our understanding would end in something far vaguer and looser than what our observation began with. Aristotle at least could refer particulars to their specific types, as medicine and social science are still glad enough to do, to help them in guessing and in making a learned show before the public. But if divination and eloquence—for science is out of the question—were to invoke nothing but a fluid tendency to grow, we should be left with a flat history of phenomena and no means of prediction or even classification. All knowledge would be reduced to gossip, infinitely diffuse, perhaps enlisting our dramatic feelings, but yielding no intellectual mastery of experience, no practical competence, and no moral lesson. The world would be a serial novel, to be continued forever, and all men mere novel readers."[8]

A Harmony Due to Identity of Impulsion

Having rejected both radical mechanism and radical finalism, Bergson attributes those harmonies in nature that have furnished materials for the teleological argument of theology to an identity of impulsion rather than to an aspiration after any future goal existent in the mind of a Creator. He says: "If the evolution of life is something other than a series of adaptations to accidental circumstances, so also it is not the realization of a plan. A plan is given in advance. It is represented, or at least representable, before its realization."[9]

---

[8] Santayana, Winds of Doctrine, p. 68.

[9] Creative Evolution, p. 52.

Such harmony, he concludes, would be won only at the expense of freedom. "If, on the contrary, the unity of life is to be found solely in the impetus that pushes it along the road of time, the harmony is not in front, but behind."[10]

At this point we ought to stop and take inventory of our ideas to be saved from being swept along on the wave of undefined terms. What do we mean by unity of life? Is the "impetus" something that survives the passage of time and events. If there is to be a continuity in an impetus, something must keep its identity. Just what would the identity of a changing impetus be? We cannot have identity without something to be identical. To have consciousness of change there must be an abiding element that survives change. Personality is the only reality in life which we can actually posit as causing or experiencing change and yet itself maintaining its identity. Is the "vital impulse," then, an unchanging personality? If it is not (and we are given no such clue to its nature), then all must have

---

[10] Creative Evolution, p. 103.

been set going in some past time. In that case we have not escaped from the closed system Bergson seeks to avoid, but have, rather, fallen back into the pit. If it is not a personality, and yet acts in the present in lives so diverse as Mr. Bergson's and mine, of what does the unity consist?

Out of this positing of the "vital impetus" grows Bergson's definition of God: "God has nothing of the already made; he is unceasing life, action, freedom. Creation, so conceived, is not a mystery; we experience it ourselves when we act freely."[11]

By this definition he hopes to escape the dilemma just mentioned. This is because he senses the fact that his problem cannot be met on the impersonal plane. It remains to inquire if the God of his definition is sufficient for the need. To provide the necessary impetus we have a growing, changing, becoming God. The question at once arises as to how a becoming God, who is himself a part of the general movement, could, with a constantly changing mind, outlook, and purpose, furnish an identity of impulsion.

[11] Creative Evolution, pp. 104, 105.

Where are we to find the looked-for harmony? Will the harmony be for this day, this hour, or this minute? It includes all? Then we cannot avoid pantheism, and every kind of impulse, criminal and saintly, the strange gamut of human heroism and beastliness, are a part of God and issue from the "vital impetus." We have crawled in by the cellar window to find ourselves once more in the pent-up quarters of Absolutism, out of the front door of which we recently marched with drums beating and banners flaunting. What Eucken says of the spiritual life is here equally applicable to the thought of a becoming God: "Spiritual life must never be understood as an entire Becoming—as a mere Process—for, if this were the case, Truth would become the mere slave of its age; and such a state of things would mean an inner destruction of Truth."[12] In the same way a becoming God falls prey to his own creation, is no God.

But Bergson's object in positing a God is to provide a ground of duration which shall

[12] Eucken, Knowledge and Life, p. 228.

158

include all human experiences of duration.
We have already noted the timeless element
necessary to all consciousness of change. If
we are to have a God who will be a real
Ground, he must himself be more than a
creation of time, else there is nothing in the
thought of duration as Bergson employs the
term. But we cannot admit the assumption of a God not a creation of time without
being led far afield from Bergson's standpoint. Bowne has well expressed the relation of the Supreme Being to time in his
discussion of the Kantian philosophy:

"The bringing of the present with the
resultant time judgment into relation to
activity greatly modifies the subject. We
call those things present which we possess
in the certain immediacy of consciousness,
and if we possessed all our experiences in a
similar immediacy, the whole experience
would be present in the same sense. There
would still be a certain order of arrangement
among the factors of experience which could
not arbitrarily be modified, but all the mem-
bers of the series would be equally present
to the consciousness. If, now, there were a

being who could retain all the facts of his experience in the same immediacy, he would have no past. And, further, if such a being were in full possession of himself, so as to be under no law of development and possessing no unrealized potentialities, he would also have no future, at least so far as his own existence might be concerned. His present world would be all-embracing, and his now would be eternal. These considerations modify our judgment of the subjectivity of time very profoundly. Taking up once more the question, Are we in time? we see that it has several meanings and the answers must vary to correspond. If it means, Are things and events in a real time which flows on independently of them? the answer must be, No. If it means, Does our experience have the temporal form? the answer must be, Yes. If we further inquire about the possibility of transcending temporal limitations, it is clear that this can be affirmed only of the Absolute Being, for only in him do we find that complete self-possession which the transcendence of time would mean. Nontemporality, then, in the concrete sense cannot be reached by passing behind the world of phenomena into the world of noumena, but, rather, and only by rising above the sphere of the finite into the absolute self-possession of the infinite."[13]

Bergson lacks what Bowne had so clearly, a Personal World-Ground, himself the unchanging Cause of change. Bergson leaves out of reckoning that purpose which makes humanity great. For man is indeed great in the universe and the lord of all only as behind his little and short-sighted purpose lies a deeper Purpose which is also a Person.

In this connection my attention has been called to a letter written by Mr. Bergson to Father Joseph de Tonquedec, S. J., and quoted in a recent review of Bergson's philosophy:[14]

"I speak of God (pp. 268–272 of L'Evolution Creatrice) as of the *source* whence issue successively, by an effect of his freedom, the 'currents' or 'impulses' each of which will make a world; he therefore, re-

---

[13] Bowne, Kant and Spencer, pp. 158, 159.

[14] Ruhe and Paul, Henri Bergson, an Account of his Life and Philosophy, p. 42.

mains distinct from them, and it is not of him that we can say that 'most often it turns aside' or it is 'at the mercy of the materiality that it has been bound to adopt.' " . . . Again he is quoted as saying: "From all this emerges clearly the idea of a God, Creator and free, the generator of both matter and life, whose work of creation is continued on the side of life by the evolution of species and the building up of human personalities. From all this emerges, consequently, a refutation of monism and of pantheism in general."[15]

The reply to this is that if Mr. Bergson wishes to hold to this conception of God, he must modify his system. He here assumes that God is made free by fiat. This statement does not remove the yoke of necessity which must ever hang about the neck of a Being whose mind, thought, and moral character are in process of becoming—that is, who is himself a creature of time. It is not enough to affirm that God always existed. We must go still further and ask what he was at first. In the case of a be-

---

[15] Ibid., p. 44.

coming God he may not have been God in the beginning. He may have grown to that estate. Mental and moral perfection and timelessness, in other words, are necessary to our thought of God. A lesser Being may be a blind demiurge, but possessing no personality, becomes inevitably the victim of his own world. If Mr. Bergson wishes to avoid a pantheistic God, it devolves upon him to modify his philosophy, and to so clear his definitions that a pantheistic God will not be implied.

His Doctrine of Knowledge

We must not leave this brief review of Bergson's system without looking at his doctrine of intelligence and intuition as contrasting forms of knowledge. He suggests that intuition really gets nearer to life, while intellect is, by the nature of the mind, bound to the rigors of geometrical explanation. The knowledge gained by intuition is, however, intensive, and applicable only in a realm of limited life. But intelligence is able to transcend itself: "There are things that intelligence alone is able to seek, but which, by itself, it will never find. These things instinct alone could find; but it will never seek them."[16]

Intuition leads us to the very inwardness of life. Intelligence, however, had the ability to turn inward on itself and to "awaken the potentialities of intuition which slumber within it."[17] Intuition "is a lamp almost extinguished, which only glimmers now and then, for a few moments at most. But it glimmers wherever a vital interest is at stake. On our personality, on our liberty, on the place we occupy in the whole of nature, on our origin, and perhaps also on our destiny, it throws a light feeble and vacillating, but none the less pierces the darkness of the night in which the intellect leaves us. . . . Philosophy introduces us thus into the spiritual life. And it shows us at the same time the relation of the life of the spirit to that of the body. . . . A philosophy of intuition will be a negation of science, will be sooner or later swept away by science, if it does not resolve to see the

[16] Creative Evolution, p. 151.
[17] Ibid., p. 182.

life of the body just where it really is, on the road that leads to the life of the spirit. But it will then no longer have to do with definite living beings. Life as a whole from the initial impulsion that thrust it into the world will appear as a wave which rises, and which is opposed by the descending movement of matter. On the greater part of its surface, at different heights, the current is converted by matter into a vortex. At one point alone it passes freely, dragging with it the obstacle which will weigh on its progress, but will not stop it. At this point is humanity; it is our privileged situation. On the other hand, this rising wave is consciousness, and, like all consciousness, it includes potentialities without number which interpenetrate and to which consequently neither the category of unity nor that of multiplicity is appropriate, made as they both are for inert matter. The matter that it bears along with it and in the interstices of which it inserts itself, alone can divide it into distinct individualities. On flows the current, running through human generations, subdividing itself into individuals. This subdivision was vaguely indicated in it, but could not have been made clear without matter. Thus souls are continually being created, which neverthe-less, in a certain sense, preexisted. . . . All the living hold together, and all yield to the same tremendous push. The animal takes its stand on the plant, man bestrides animality, and the whole of humanity, in space and in time, is one immense army galloping beside and before and behind each of us in an overwhelming charge able to beat down every resistance and clear the most formid-able obstacles, perhaps even death."[18]

It seems a pity to disturb the grandeur of words that for abstraction would do credit to the absolute philosophy itself. Out of the mazes two pertinent questions arise. The first has respect to the intuitive nature of religion and its contrast with anything in-tellectual. If intuitive knowledge is closer to life, and religion is grasped by intuition alone, why does not the savage possess the highest form of religion? To ask this ques-tion is to perceive its answer. To follow

---

[18] Creative Evolution, pp. 269–271.

reason in religion instead of blind impulse is to be moral and to attain the highest reaches of character. Religion without the intellectual content has ever proved unworthy and inadequate. Furthermore, if we are to posit any reality in "the life of the spirit," we must provide some ground for it in the "vital impulse" with its essence of Becoming. If we do this, we shall have a God who is only growing from wickedness to righteousness, and we obtain a reversal of moral standards and responsibilities.

The second question arises out of the statement that the life of the spirit will "no longer have to do with definite living being." We at once ask what such a life of the spirit would mean, and what it would amount to if it meant anything. By the definition it could mean nothing for human beings; and if it meant anything to God or to the "vital impulse," we would have no means of ascertaining. All of which goes to show that we have been regaled with a form of words and a sound of wisdom.

That Bergson has done a real service to philosophy by calling attention to intelligence and intuition as contrasting forms of knowledge cannot be gainsaid. The idea is vast in its possibility of explaining the abnormalities of genius, the uniqueness of Jesus, the authority of divine revelation, and the possibility of revelation to those who, untrained in the schools, are yet open to the deepest voices of our being. Bergson's proclamation of the value of the common intuitions, the possibility of the possession of the deepest insights by the unlettered, is one of the things that have drawn to him great popular attention. But that his ideas lack the metaphysical grounding that would make them most effective must be admitted. The truth of this statement will never be more evident than upon comparison of the abstractions of Bergson's impersonalism with the directness of Bowne's personalism.

CHAPTER XI

EUCKEN—THE RETURN TO SPIRITUAL VERITY

So many excellent expositions and reviews of the important work of this leading thinker of the present time have already appeared that it is here unnecessary to do more than touch upon the few leading features of his system in order to gather the affinity and relationship of his thought with that of Bowne.

The two thinkers possess essential features in common. There was between them the warmest personal regard and mutual appreciation. Their harmony was arrived at quite independently, though both had been pupils of Lotze. We are told that the young Eucken was not favorably impressed with Lotze, and after a short time at Göttingen passed on to another university. On the other hand, Bowne is most often known for his likeness to his former teacher. The similarities between Bowne and Eucken, however, lie, rather, along the line of the positions to which Bowne advanced independently of Lotze. The strength of the latter lay, rather, in his dialectic and in his power of clear criticism than in constructiveness and advance.

REALITY MUST INCLUDE MORE THAN THINGS, AND MORE THAN IDEAS

Eucken opposes the pretensions of the naturalistic school to include the whole world in the experience of phenomena, which leads direct to skepticism and the denial of knowledge. He also takes issue with the Absolute Philosophy, which would confine all truth to vague and shadowy ideas. He will not deny reality to the objective world, nor will he allow that the world of thought is of itself complete. He points, rather, to the value of the ideal as something toward which man may bend his energies in achievement. It is possible for intellect to arrive at great and inspiring ideals, but these find content and value only as they are achieved. He points out the impossibility of moral victory and of progress in history and civilization, if man is to be left at the dead level of a phenomenal and disunited world. It is the power of intellectual synthesis which enables man to apprehend truth and then by actual struggle to make the truth his own in character. In this "activism" Eucken would unite the subjective and objective worlds, the clue to whose relationship he finds in the life of the spirit. The spiritual in man is thus seen as something not so indefinite as to be a mere bringer of individual peace and comfort, as has often been the case with the followers of absolutism. Nothing is really had apart from struggle and the realization of the ideal in life. Spiritual truth, from being a wandering child of intellect or emotion, becomes a fundamental fact, the fundamental reality, for in its outworking it is the highest expression of man's very being.

TRUTH MUST HAVE A COMMON VALIDITY

Though insisting that ideal truth must find its value and verification in actual living, Eucken would resent being classed as a pragmatist according to the type of William James. He saves his pragmatic test of the reality of the ideal from falling into the pluralistic confusion of the latter by asserting the universal validity of truth. Truth has an authoritative validity far above the power of individual thought or caprice. James' repugnance to all general ideas and to all absolute standards led him to a view of truth which made it the victim of the individual notion, the individual himself being the sole judge of what is useful, good, and, therefore, true. No one has shown more clearly than Eucken the absurdity and worthlessness of a truth whose only norm is its utility for the individual on a given occasion. To make the truth thus the prey of individual choices, of individual standards of judgment and states of civilization, is to destroy its own inner character. So while bringing all ideals to the pragmatic test of action, he would claim for them a validity outlasting the moment of realization by a single individual. The great norms of truth lift themselves up like mountains in the moral consciousness of men as something worthy to be achieved, and will ever so lift themselves, independent of the moral failure to achieve, either on the part of any one man, or of any class of men, or of an epoch or an age. Thus Eucken assumes theism as the very ground of truth.

"We look at nature very differently from our forefathers. It no longer seems to us a realm of soulful harmony and blessed peace, but, rather, a complex riddle, the arena on which a perpetual struggle for existence is being enacted. Men too, in the wild vortex of political and social struggles, lose the romantic glory of former days; and even the exaltation of personality so usual to-day, of its grandeur, dignity, and so on—unless grounded on something greater and deeper —becomes merely a hollow and irrelevant phrase, especially in an age which so forces upon our notice the smallness and self-seeking of man. As things stand the only choice is between theism and atheism."[1]

EUCKEN'S PERSONAL IDEALISM, THE REALIZATION OF THE LIFE OF THE SPIRIT

It will be readily seen that Eucken's interests lie naturally with idealism in that he

---

[1] Eucken, Can We Still Be Christians? p. 144.

defends and maintains the necessity of the ideal to all true progress. He does not thereby, however, commit himself to that system of necessity in which intellectualism finds itself. Reality lies, not in the Divine as a passive thing, but, rather, in its realization, in its springing into action in the concrete. At the same time that he thus makes place for freedom and initiative he escapes that pantheism into which absolute idealism inevitably falls. The only difference here between Eucken and Bowne is one of emphasis rather then essence.

Bowne brings his thought to great clearness and definiteness by gathering it up into his definition of personality. The difference is not constitutional. It has been Bowne's distinctive task to develop the idea of personality. Eucken's peculiar work has been to emphasize the place and reality of the life of the spirit.

THE ABSENCE OF THE CHRISTOLOGICAL INTEREST

There is at one point an essential difference between Bowne and Eucken. This is

at the point which affects the Christological
interest, which is a very important part of
Bowne's system. With Eucken, the appearance of the Deity in a historic point of time,
speaking likewise an eternal message, is unthinkable. The realization of the moral
idea agrees inevitably with a slow advance
toward such an ideal. The ideal itself is
affected by its realization. Any revelation
of a perfect ideal in a historic personality
seems to him to put a stop to struggle and
progress. To him such revelation is incon-
gruous with imperfect human comprehension and achievement. Eucken himself tells
us of the impossibility of the atheistic standpoint and assumes theism as the necessary
moral grounding of the ideal which lifts it
above the individual judgments and ca-
prices of men to universal validity. To
Bowne this very view would demand the
incarnation for its completion. Eucken has
spoken of love as a manifestation of this
universally valid moral ideal. Yet it would
be impossible in a world of pain and error,
of human vanity and failure, of ruthless and
crushing brute force, to conceive of love as

the possession of the Supreme Moral Being
unless we had been directed to it through
the life of Jesus himself. The incarnation
becomes in the experience of man the most
effective spur to the realization of that ideal.
The deity of Jesus hinges upon this moral
necessity. We have again and again in
human history the example of men in a
supreme self-renunciation giving their lives
for the realization of the higher moral aims
and happiness of their fellow men. What
shall we conclude concerning a magnified
personality, the abode of absolute ideals,
who can do no more than give advice by
which to offset the disheartening evils and
the crushing sorrows of the world? Without
an incarnation man would himself be capable of a moral grandeur and outlook of
which God would give no evidence. The
incarnation is necessary to save the thought
of moral perfection in God. An incarnation
past or an incarnation to come would seem
to Bowne to be implied by the demands of
thought.

"If God had filled space and time with
inanimate worlds, that would have revealed

only power and skill. If he had filled the world with pleasure-giving contrivances, that would have revealed benevolence. If he had sent us prophets and teachers at no real cost to himself, that too would be something; but it would not greatly stir our hearts toward God. Our love would go out to the prophets and teachers themselves, for the toil and pain would fall on them. In all beneficence of this sort God would appear simply as a rich man who out of his abundance scatters bounty to the needy, but at no cost to himself. A certain gratitude would indeed be possible, but along this line God would forever remain morally below the moral heroes of our race. Their gifts cost. They put themselves and their hearts into their work. They attain to the morality of self-sacrifice, and this is infinitely beyond the morality of any giving that does not cost. And there must ever be a higher moral possibility until we reach the revelation of God in self-sacrifice, until God becomes the chief of burden-bearers and the leader of all in self-abnegation. . . . Thus the power of God's revelation has its chief source in the incarnation. And we may be perfectly sure that no lower conception of God will permanently command the minds and hearts of men. We should not have reached the conception ourselves, but now that it has been revealed to us, we see that something of the kind is a moral necessity if we are to think the highest thought of God. And there is a peculiar dialectic in human thought whereby we are compelled to think of God as perfect or not at all. An imperfect God is none. As soon as a higher conception emerges we must adopt it into our thought of God or see our faith in him fade out until it vanishes altogether. A fairly good God we cannot abide. We can be satisfied with nothing less than the supreme and the perfect. Hence it is that the Christian thought of God wins its way. It is the only one worthy of God or man."[2]

How God could empty himself to become a partaker in human toils and sorrows will remain, of course, inexplicable. It will also remain beyond our comprehension how a

[2] Bowne, Studies in Christianity, pp. 96, 104.

178

timeless personality could reveal himself to any part of his world in any degree, or, in revealing the moral ideal to man, consent to work under the limitations of time. The particular ground of this difficulty is in the confusing of the power world with the space and time world.

If, however, the debate should rage about the thought of the possession by the historic Jesus in the flesh of all the divine powers and attributes in order to establish his Deity, we have recourse to the theory of the Kenosis. We believe his deity is sufficiently verified by the revelation of perfect moral character which formed the supreme object of his revelation. The deity of Jesus is proved neither by genealogy nor miracle in themselves.

The character and personality of Jesus is the world's great miracle. The most convincing test for the present age is to be found in the essentially universal mastership of the character of Jesus, and his ability to satisfy the moral and spiritual demands of all classes and conditions of men. No other man, prophet or hero, ever lived that could for any length of time, for all races of man, fulfill in his own character their highest ideal of the character of God. Eucken speaks of him as classified with other great geniuses. Viewed from the single standpoint of his teaching of moral truth, this might be. One might come with transcendent spiritual insight to do for the realm of religion what Shakespeare and Mozart have done in the realm of literature and music. But great genius has too often been commonplace in morals and in ideals. There is no certainty that a future age may not produce a greater master than either. The love and the passion of Jesus, his revelation of the moral character of God, can never be transcended so long as humanity shall retain its essential nature. But Jesus is much more than the teacher of a truth which has not been transcended. In the case of spiritual revelation, the personality of the teacher is quite as important as his message. Not only are his truths compelling for all classes of men, his personality has never been transcended as the supreme goal of man's achievement. He thus remains undimmed above the march of ages, and every moral advance of the race but serves to increase the appreciation in which he is held. The actual test between Jesus and other geniuses is to be found in his character, in himself. His deity is to be read in the universal compulsion and validity of his order of life. Incarnation is the easiest and most satisfying explanation of the character of Jesus. All others break down.

Disagreement with his Christological views is likely to blind the eyes of many of the most conscientious to the greatness and the importance to religion of the work of Rudolf Eucken. He easily represents the supreme philosophical message of our day, and his constructive work and leadership promises to wield a profound influence in the cause of faith. His voice comes to his time like that of one of the Hebrew prophets, when the age engrossed in the pursuit of material things was forgetting that it had a soul at all. He speaks to an age that in its scientific thinking has steadily barred out the spiritual as an illusion and a dream. He speaks to a world of philosophy which

to a large degree has lost its way in the
meshes of skepticism and materialism. And
his word is ever for the reality of the higher
things of the spirit, in behalf of the necessity for the moral regeneration of man, and
the life that is lived in conscious harmony
with God. He shows in phrases of beauty
and convincing power that though a man
possess the whole world, if he loses his own
soul he has utterly failed. For back of all
our getting and enjoying the fundamental
truth of life is the spiritual. Adapting an
old, old thought, the chief end of man is
the realization of God.

CHAPTER XII

BOWNE'S PERSONALISM AND THE PROBLEMS OF LIFE

AT the risk of repetition, it may be well to touch upon the relation of Personalism to some of the problems of life. Bowne saw, as few others, how impossible it is to account for an intelligible and orderly world, for knowledge and for spiritual reality, on the plane of the impersonal. This was his distinctive contribution to philosophy. So clear was his criticism along this line that all metaphysical thinking will be forced to take account of it.

UNITY POSSIBLE ONLY THROUGH PERSONALISM

Personalism is the most reasonable solution of the problem of unity. A unity obtained by assuming a unitary substance must inevitably negate the reality of knowledge, mind, and spirit. A unity which is won by lifting time and space into realities

independent of all intelligence, involves
confusion no less than that of materialism.
Time as duration cannot be thought without a clearly defined personality which is
more than consciousness, more than memory,
self-directing and free. Change and identity
are irreconcilable except through an abiding
Personality surviving above their fluctua-
tions. A unity obtained by assuming an
Absolute of whose thought the world is but
the outworking, ends in a pantheism fatal
to all freedom or individuality. If instead
of naming a vague Absolute as the ground
of all things, we assume a free Personality
upholding the world of things, and the
world of spirits endowed by him with a
freedom akin to his own, then all is well.
There exists, then, no insoluble problem of
how the mind can grasp matter or of how its
knowledge can represent reality. It is no
longer necessary to attempt the tracing of
matter and motion and molecular change
into the brain cells to account for an idea
of beauty or an aspiration of the soul after
God. We note for scientific or pathological
purposes the physical changes and the psy-

chological results, but we no longer dream that we have grasped all the factors in the process, nor do we relegate to the realm of unreality all that our investigation fails to explain. We think truly of the world of matter because the world of matter is founded in an Intelligence related to our own. The mind and the world are by their very nature prepared to correspond and co-operate, and both find synthesis and agreement in that intelligent Personality which is able to grasp all and to act in all.

There is no longer a conflict between science and religion, because the laws of nature are seen as the self-imposed ways of the Divine in bringing forth the order of change. Natural laws are not erected into an independent system in which God is a slave, for they are but the uniformities of his activity. The deductions which we draw from the order of sequence are not to be given a causal efficiency.

Personalism and Freedom

We thus come to the problem of freedom and necessity. Freedom is not provided for

in any naturalistic scheme whatever. This
is not alone because of innate or *a priori*
ideas which cannot be traced to experience.
It is not merely inability to trace the
products of reflection to appropriate nervous
excitations. The power of self-directing personality to introduce its own will as a new
factor into the order of nature is too evident
in common experience to be overlooked.
This introduction of purpose to modify the
natural processes is something of which
nature herself is evidently incapable. The
mechanical system of causation would not
only deprive man of individuality, but
would preclude the possibility of moral
action.

The outcome of absolutism of the extreme
type is very close to that of materialism
despite their wide difference of spirit and of
aim. Absolutism, seeing in all a manifestation of the Divine Idea, cannot escape making God a moral monster, responsible for
the weaknesses, errors, and sins of men.
By the same token man would be no longer
morally responsible, because he would not be
free. He would be but the unresisting tool

through which the Divine works sometimes good and sometimes ill.

On the personal plane we can affirm a good and perfect God who has given to man a personality measurably like his own, free to act in accordance with or against the Divine will. Moral action is of like nature in God and man, being voluntarily chosen in distinction from wrong. Man becomes thus morally responsible, and his freedom to make a confusion of God's world is a gift to which he is to be held strictly to account. He is no longer to be considered as giving forth the thoughts and activities to which he is compelled by physical environment, nor is he an automaton, finding all his thoughts of holiness or wickedness inspired by the Eternal, the manifestations of whose thought under the absolutist scheme, they would be.

PERSONALISM AND THE PROBLEM OF EVIL

The schools of idealism and of materialism find equal difficulty when they face the problem of evil. If one were compelled to choose between the two, the dilemma which they present is this: either a God who is as responsible for evil as he is for good, or a world that is essentially unmoral. In either case it would be impossible to hold to individual moral responsibility. No doubt if all the wrong that springs from immoral thinking and acting were eliminated, the great mass of evil that depresses man and creates his problem would be done away. Still there would remain the mysteries of pain and death, and for these it would at first seem almost impossible to clear the Infinite Personality. This point is the rock on which theism is supposed to wreck itself.

One thing is certain: there can be no satisfactory solution for human spirits along the line of blind, purposeless, impersonal causation. If our sorrows, griefs, and ills are not for discipline after some manner, we have simply to cry into the dark. We may not be able to satisfy our minds, but we certainly cannot satisfy our souls except through assuming a divine purpose which works good in our behalf through pain. When to the demand of our spirits we add the consciousness of our limitations in knowledge and our lack of understanding of disciplines which have afterward proved the most substantial blessings, we can see how an Intelligence not bound to the temporal form of experience, seeing the end from the beginning, in view of the moral discipline attained, might account the whole course as very good. Why discipline should be necessary is a question bound up with that of the attainment of character. That it is necessary is a commonplace of experience.

If the further question of the suffering of the innocent for the guilty is invoked, we can only say that, in such a case, suffering is a contribution to the moral progress of the world. Voluntarily accepted, it becomes to the sufferer, by that strange mystery of personality, the deepest and most satisfying joy that life can give. If to this thought should be added the thought of the Creator of all entering with moral fullness into human life and giving himself for the moral welfare of his creatures, we should at once make possible the maintenance of theism in the face of the problem of evil. This assumption would also be in strict keeping

with the deepest facts of religion and of life.
In the world around us we begin to see

> On every side
> Great hints of Him go by—
> Souls that are hourly crucified
> On some new Calvary!
>
> .   .   .   .
>
> In flower and dust, in chaff and grain,
> He binds Himself and dies!
> We live by His eternal pain,
> His hourly sacrifice.[3]

What of death, that last but not most
inexplicable of mysteries? No man who
has had wide experience of life is unaware
that in a world of physical and moral in-
firmity there frequently arise situations to
which death itself is a welcome relief. Here,
as before, there is no explanation on the
impersonal plane. The world has too often
witnessed the cynicism and moral flabbiness
of those who assume that there is no sur-
vival of death. That assumption has long
been proved as not the road that leads to
high moral achievement and the enrich-
ment of life with things most precious. So

[3] Noyes, "Vicisti Galileæ," Collected Poems, vol. i, p. 244.

much there is for the practical side of the argument.

On the theoretical side is still another consideration. In our knowledge we are shut up to the present order of existence. We cannot look at life from the standpoint of any other order. It might be that to see it from another order would transmute death into blessed good fortune, the thing most to be desired. It might indeed, be found that

> "Death is but a change of key,
> In life the golden melody."

On the personal plane, then, if we can trust the wisdom of the Supreme Personal Intelligence, even the last of the dark problems, if not finding abstract solution, may yet find one sufficient for the individual need. Even Henley, with his sense of pessimism, could come to look on death with complacency as the benediction of a departing day, thrilled with the sense of the triumphing night,

> Night with her train of stars
> And her great gift of sleep.

In this mood he could pray with a steady courage,

"So be my passing!
My task accomplished and the long day done,
        My wages taken, and in my heart
        Some late lark singing."

Here too he came to look for the solution of earthly misunderstanding and irreconcilable ills as voiced in lines said to have been addressed to Robert Louis Stevenson:

O Death and Time they chime and chime
Like bells at sunset falling!
They end the song, they right the wrong,
    They set the old echoes calling:
For Death and Time bring on the prime
    Of God's own chosen weather,
And we lie in the peace of the Great Release
    As once in the grass together.

It is not only impossible to face the problem of evil with any satisfaction apart from the personalistic view. The problem can never be solved in the abstract. It must be solved in each particular case as it arises. In some cases this seems quite impossible, but in most death comes as a benevolence to the individual, second only to birth itself. For, after all, the value of a life is not determined by its length, but by its realization of the highest things.

Let the great winds their worst and wildest blow,
Or the gold weather mellow round us slow:
We have fulfilled ourselves, and we can dare
And we can conquer.

Personality is surely the richest gift of man, and who can deny that it is likewise the supreme possession of God?

Mr. James has said in his Pluralistic Universe: "A man's vision is the great fact about him. A philosophy is the expression of a man's intimate character, and all the definitions of the universe are but the deliberately adopted reactions of human characters upon it." This was particularly true of Bowne. It, as much as his philosophy, was the source of his deep and widening influence. Men gathered from east and west to hear his teaching with varying preparation and adaptability for philosophical endeavor. The intellectual rewards which they carried away were as varied as the men who came, but all had this in common: each was certain that he had felt the touch of a master spirit. They were one in a feeling of exaltation and inspiration. Wherever they have gone to the various tasks of business or professional life, or social ministry, they have gone even to the ends of the earth in a new, high sense of the greatness and meaning of life and with a loyalty that time cannot dim. If two such meet in the antipodes, the common meeting ground is "Did you take Bowne's work?" The underlying significance of all this is the inspiration of an unusual personality, a mind that rang so true that it satisfied the most questioning youth, a vision and an insight which lifted the student into the heights and enabled him to grasp the relations of life to the world, to man, and to God. Accused by the shallow-minded of heresy, the strong religious tone of all Bowne's teaching was its predominant characteristic. This was the very point most criticized by his philosophical contemporaries, to whom the recognition of religious verity was a sign of philosophical weakness. The religious note was never wanting as he unfolded to his eager students the thought of the great minds of the centuries. Never did he fail to draw them in perspective to the thought of One who was his Master. We

"Watched the great hills, like clouds arise and set;
And one named Olivet"

was never missing from the horizon.

For this reason he was at the close of life fitted as perhaps no other man of his time for great constructive religious and intellectual leadership. He was already beginning to influence profoundly the thought of the Orient as he had already influenced many in the West. It was his distinction to be almost better known in Germany than at home. His loyalty to an institution kept him from entering into that large measure of recognition that might have come to him earlier. So far as human judgment can discern, he is gone too soon. But his work will live. It was done so truly, so conscientiously, so greatly, that its influence is certain to deepen with the passing years. This will prove true in that age which we feel is just at hand, when men will more generally recognize the inadequacy of great thinking which is lacking in reverence and respect for the profounder realities and problems of our mortal life. There is that in the work of Bowne that answers to the deepest spiritual questionings, and in death as in life he can await the judgment of the years unhumiliated and unafraid.

BIBLIOGRAPHY

Included in this list are the titles which have been found most helpful in the particular field covered. It does not aim to be exhaustive.

GENERAL

Adamson, Development of Modern Philosophy.
Bowne, Metaphysics.
Bowne, Personalism.
Bowne, Philosophy of Theism.
Bowne, Studies in Christianity.
Bowne, The Essence of Religion.
Bowne, Theory of Thought and Knowledge.
Caird, Problems of Philosophy at the Present Time.
Dewing, Introduction to the History of Modern Philosophy.
Eucken, The Problem of Human Life.
Höffding, History of Modern Philosophy.
Janet and Sailles, History of the Problems of Philosophy.
Külpe, Philosophy of the Present in Germany.
Pfleiderer, Philosophy and Development of Religion.
Windelband, History of Philosophy.

BIBLIOGRAPHY

ANCIENT PHILOSOPHY

Adamson, Development of Greek Philosophy.
Aristotle, Logic.
Aristotle, Metaphysics.
Eucken, Fundamental Concepts of Modern Thought.
Eucken, Life's Basis and Life's Ideal.
Gompers, Greek Thinkers.

MATERIALISM

Bowne, Kant and Spencer.
Eucken, The Truth of Religion.
Höffding, Influence of the Conception of Evolution.
Lange, History of Materialism.

KANT

Bowne, Kant and Spencer.
Kant, Critique of Pure Reason.
Stahlin, Kant, Lotze, and Ritschl (Reply to Lange, Materialism).

LOTZE

Caspari, Hermann Lotze, etc., pp. 4 and 53.
Falckenberg, Hermann Lotze.
Jones, Critical Account of the Philosophy of Lotze.
Külpe, Philosophy of the Present in Germany (Lotze chapter).
Lotze, Metaphysics.
Lotze, Microcosmus.
Pfleiderer, Lotze's philosophische Weltanschauung nach ihren Grundzugen. (Sympathetic treatment.)

BIBLIOGRAPHY

Schiller, Humanism (Reference to Lotze).
Seth, Development from Kant to Hegel.

PRAGMATISM

Bawden, Principles of Pragmatism.
Berthelot, Un Romantisme utilitaire (Volume II contains exhaustive treatment of Bergson's Pragmatism).
Davidson, The Stoic Creed.
De Laguna, Dogmatism and Evolution.
Haldane, Pathway to Reality.
James, Essays in Radical Empiricism.
James, Pluralistic Universe.
James, Pragmatism.
James, Problems of Philosophy.
James, Will to Believe.
Jourdain, Theory of the Infinite in Modern Thought.
Lyman, Influence of Pragmatism on Theology.
Parker, Plato and Pragmatism (short essay, but very good).
Schiller, Humanism.
Schiller, Riddles of the Sphinx (3rd edition).
Schinz, Anti-pragmatism.
Vernon Lee, Vital Lies.

BERGSON

Bergson, Creative Evolution.
Bergson, Introduction to Metaphysics (Article, Metaphysical and Moral Revelation, January, '03).

BIBLIOGRAPHY

Bergson, Matter and Memory.

Bergson, The Immediate Data of Consciousness.

Bergson, Time and Free Will.

Hermann, Eucken and Bergson.

James, Pluralistic Universe, Chapter VI.

Le Roy, New Philosophy of Bergson.

Ruhe and Paul, Henri Bergson, An Account of His
Life and Personality.

Solomon, Bergson.

EUCKEN

Eucken, Life's Basis and Life's Ideal.

Eucken, Main Currents of Modern Thought.

Eucken, Problem of Human Life.

Eucken, The Life of the Spirit.

Eucken, The Truth of Religion.

Gibson, Eucken's Philosophy of Life.

Hermann, Eucken and Bergson.

INDEX

201

INDEX

INDEX

INDEX

INDEX

INDEX

INDEX